4/10/14

To Roberta,

All the best in
life — always Phyllis

M000170104

Fired at

50

A Survivor's Guide
to Prosperity

Phyllis Green

Fired at Fifty: A Survivor's Guide to Prosperity

Copyright © 2014 by Phyllis Green
Published 2014 by Teramar Media, Inc.
West Palm Beach, FL USA

All rights reserved. No part of this book may be used or reproduced in any manner whatsoever without written permission except in the case of brief quotations embodied in critical articles and review.

ISBN: 978-0-9914759-0-2

Edited by Margarita Pardo Abrishami
Cover Illustration by Octavio Guzman

I GRATEFULLY DEDICATE THIS BOOK TO my loving family and all the changes we have experienced together. My amazing and exceptional children, Steven and Suzanne, helped me survive the loss of their brother, Robert, my eldest child. Their caring love and friendship have guided me through the years.

I am blessed to share my life's experiences with my four impressive grandchildren: Juli, Devon, David, and Ben, and my wonderful son-in-law, Glenn.

Lastly, my life has been enriched by the wisdom and guidance of Bren, my BFF, and Howard, my nephew and best friend.

Contents

Part One
The Career Track

Part Two
The Shake-Up

Part Three
The Entrepreneur

Part Four

How to Sell When You're on Top

Part Five

The Next Transition

Part Six

Let's Take It Personal

Introduction

Every person, from eight to eighty and beyond, experiences life-altering events that change them forever: the first day at school, that first week in a new job situation, a new marriage, a first child, moving to a new city, or even another country. The commonality in these experiences is change. This book deals with change, the universal experience for each of us.

Fired at Fifty is symbolic in nature: a metaphor for a major life-altering event. As a metaphor, many of these experiences and interactions with colleagues, mentors, the famous and the not-so-famous can be translated to your more personal experiences. Life is not a straight line; we encounter obstacles and challenges at every turn. Our good decisions may turn bad. A seemingly bad experience may provide a great occasion to learn a lesson. Often, our uncertainty forces us to explore a path that leads to real opportunity. There's a wise saying: "It's not what happens to us, but how we deal with what happens to us."

Each of us has more control over our lives than we can possibly imagine. A demonstration of resilience and a degree of flexibility go far in helping us handle these natural life cycles. Never underestimate your ability to transition from one cycle to the next. From twenty years of age, I experienced cycles of being hired, promoted, fired, hired, and fired again. During these passages, I remembered a famous quote from visionary dancer Martha Graham: "You are unique, and, if that is not fulfilled, then something has been lost."

My journey to entrepreneurship and beyond proved to be the fulfillment of my destiny. I hope this book will serve to guide others to reach their destiny: not only to survive the journey of life, but to thrive and prosper.

Prologue: The Three Little Words
I Never Expected to Hear

FROM THE CORNER OFFICE ON the thirtieth floor of a prestigious New York midtown office building to the whitewashed walls and shabby floors of the 18th Street New York State unemployment office, the distance is just thirty-six city blocks. Not just a world apart, the two offices could have been on different planets.

The year was 1985; life was good and I knew it. What I didn't know was how uncertain my good life was. I learned quickly that the good life and its rewards disappear on the day you are fired. That's when I began to navigate the thirty-six blocks from corporate bliss to unemployment nightmare.

How did I get here? What did I do wrong? Why didn't I see the approaching disaster scenario that would change my life forever? At the time, these negative thoughts permeated my every waking moment and intruded my sleep in the middle of the night.

I never saw it coming. I always thought that employees are fired when a company starts to lose clients or profits. I always thought that if you're making positive contributions and substantial efforts, you're rewarded with raises and promotions. What I did not know is that management can make decisions based on criteria about which you are clueless and even powerless to alter.

When Capital Cities bought the ABC Television Network, it was obvious to many that there would be immediate employee firings. Capital Cities was a lean, well-run media company, with an unflinching eye on bottom-line numbers. ABC-TV was a well-regarded company but had grown fat throughout the years and was ripe for acquisition. The three major television networks had changed hands in the same year, and the word "downsizing" appeared more frequently in the news.

> **I never saw it coming. I always thought that employees are fired when a company starts to lose clients or profits.**

My life was good. I had a personal secretary; a dandy expense account; access to corporate cars and more. In fact, my life was great; that is, until the day it abruptly ended. Cap Cities had mandated immediate personnel cuts and my position achieved the dubious honor of making the first list.

Like most corporate executives in their fifties, I had meticulously forged my career over a period of thirty years. I'd worked hard to earn tangible rewards for performance and success—the promotions, compensation, and bonuses—that went part and parcel with the job. I also enjoyed the many intangible rewards that were just as important: a sense of accomplishment, personal satisfaction, productivity, and self-worth.

Just as hundreds of thousands of people have experienced job losses in the past few years, I was suddenly unemployed. I had no job, no salary, and no prospects. The stinging embarrassment at being fired was with me every second. I answered ads, networked with friends, and reached back to all of the contacts of my thirty-year career... that is, those who would even answer my phone calls.

Up until the day I was fired, I had been working in a state of complete denial. I was nervous and scared regarding the Cap Cities acquisition. But it is human nature to hope against hope that it isn't your turn. So when the day finally came, I was not prepared to hear the solemn and final bad news.

"You are fired."

But wait, I'm getting ahead of my own story.

Part One

THE CAREER TRACK

Back to the Future

I T WAS EARLY MORNING ON a recent birthday. I dove into the backyard pool of my Florida home for a brisk swim to energize my day. The rhythmic activity proved relaxing and my thoughts drifted effortlessly over the last twenty-plus years that had brought me to this place and this moment. Suddenly, I was propelled back to my fifties, a time when I was operating at the top of my professional game in the most competitive and exciting business environment in the world: New York City.

Flash back to the morning of my fifty-second birthday. I was barely awake, but already felt a sense of doom and gloom. It was a Thursday, and Thursdays meant going to the New York State Office of Unemployment and standing in line for more than an hour. At the front of the line was a clipboard where the unemployed attested to their job-seeking efforts during the previous week. That was it; nothing more, nothing less. Personal job counseling interviews were scheduled monthly, purportedly to encourage your employment efforts, but really just to ensure that you were still making that effort.

As I left the Office of Unemployment that day, I once again thought carefully about my future. Who would hire a woman in her fifties? How many more times would I hear the word "overqualified"? How much longer could I afford to live in New York City with my dwindling bank account? Maybe my career was over and a job at Macy's perfume counter was my destiny.

I was not alone in my misery. As conversation flowed while waiting in two-and three-hour lines each week, it was clear that many former executives earning high salaries were now my unemployment colleagues.

We shared our initial grief that evolved into numbness about our lives. Today we might identify the emotion as post-traumatic stress syndrome. Then we called it rotten luck and felt victimized. It was not a good time for middle-aged people to restart their careers.

The weekly stories we shared had a dark edge of anxiety and frustration. As each one of us looked to transition our lives with a new career, the weeks of counting unemployment checks flew by. I was one of the few that could recount the previous week's job interviews. As a recognizable name in television sales, many high-profile New York-based advertising agencies granted actual interviews. Sadly, some of these interviews were not for real jobs, but more for learning how the TV networks and their owned-stations priced their inventory. (Inventory in media-

> **The realization hit me that there would not be a straight path to any future success.**

land is commercial airtime, such as thirty-second TV spots, ten-second intros, and more.) It's no secret that, unlike newspapers, broadcast sales seldom have an actual rate card. The cost of air-time is based upon ratings, share of market, supply and demand.

It was humbling and demeaning to leave an interview with an exciting advertising firm filled with smart, busy people, and slowly realize that your so-called job interview was a fact-finding session instead.

The realization hit me that there would not be a straight path to any future success. While some of my unemployment friends went to career counselors and began a battery of career assessment tests, I scoured the Help Wanted ads and finally found the window of opportunity that opened my world to the new world of entrepreneurism, in a most unexpected way.

I'll say more about Barter Advantage later in my story, but since every true story has a good beginning, let's begin where I started.

Ironically, it was exactly where I eventually ended up: in Florida.

These Boots Are Made for Walking...
Up the Corporate Ladder

I T WAS THE EARLY SEVENTIES. I was working at a Miami TV station as the "replacement" weather girl: this meant I was a promotional writer five days a week. However, if and when the weekend weather girl didn't show up due to an excess amount of partying, I was allowed to don my go-go boots, a nifty pair of "hot" pants and read the weather off the Teleprompter.

Looking back, it's strange to realize how different the early days of television were from where we are today. There was no security at the station. Helicopters landed and took off from the station's parking lot. And job descriptions were fluid.

One week in early January I was asked to work on a Sunday because some business clients would be visiting the station to view a football game being broadcast locally in Miami. Little did I realize that this game would be one of the most historic games in football history: Super Bowl III!

Earlier that week, quarterback Joe Namath made an appearance at the Miami Touchdown Club and brashly guar-

anteed a victory for his team. He promised a win for the
AFL New York Jets over the heavily favored NFL Baltimore
Colts. He and his team delivered. This was actually the
first Super Bowl to feature famous celebrities as entertainment instead of just college marching bands. Comedian Bob
Hope led the pre-game ceremony honoring the Apollo as-
tronauts. That historic win began the format for Super Bowl
Sunday—a national holiday in this country. As for me, I'll
never forget that Broadway Joe appeared on our TV station's sports set the next day and gave each girl a big hug
and a kiss!

So maybe Oprah Winfrey wouldn't consider my Miami
experience much of a broadcast career, but it *did* look good
on my resume. And it was good enough to get me hired by
the ABC affiliate Indianapolis TV station as associate pro-

ducer for their new, local TV talk show, slated to air within a month.

There was only one minor problem: I wasn't sure where Indiana was, and I had to drive there. To those living in the vast and lovely middle of our country, this sounds like a snobbish East Coast cliché. However, living on the eastern seaboard, it did seem that everything west of the Mississippi River was somewhere "out there." I was not fazed by this lack of information, however: I was a *problem solver*, so I turned to the weather map at the Miami TV studio to find Indiana. I started with Pennsylvania, worked my way through Ohio, and finally, there it was—Indiana!

I consoled my mother (who would be left behind) by telling her that I was *not* taking her grandchildren to the Dust Bowl, or even to the Wild West. Indeed, Indiana was practically in the *east* and just a *stone's throw* from Florida! With this little white lie, we eventually made it to Indianapolis where I started my new career at WLWI-TV.

On my first day at the station, I asked the first person I met where I could find my new office. He said, "Do I look like a traffic cop?" I was mortified, but later learned this was David Letterman's weirdly funny style of humor.

Short and Sweet

A T THE NEW DAYTIME TALK show called *The Bernie Her-man Show*, my official title may have been associate producer, but my job description was "Do whatever it takes." I helped book the B-list and C-list stars, authors, and musicians who were interested in appearing on our show to promote whatever it was that they currently needed to promote. In exchange, we filled airtime.

In those days of zero security issues, one of the more interesting parts of my job was actually transporting the guests from their hotel or airport to the TV station. I spent priceless hours of one-on-one time with many famous guests from sports to show business personalities, and even some who defied classification.

Booking a broad range of guests for a local daytime talk show proved challenging and interesting. When I contacted the late author Jimmy Breslin about his most recently published book, his first question was, "Where's Indianapolis?" He quickly added, "And wherever it is, nobody goes there, anyway!" During my stint at ABC-TV years later, I saw Jimmy several times at a New York east side bar, The Racing

Club, in which I was a minority partner. When I reminded him of our conversation back in the early seventies, he had no memory of it.

The Indy 500 racecar drivers were much more accessible, and A.J. Foyt was a personal favorite. As a tough-talking Texan, he was never at a loss for words. He would bring his most competitive buddies to the station, as they also were accomplished Indy 500 drivers. The year that Al Unser won the race he surprised everyone at the TV station by showing up unannounced with his arm around A.J. The Unser family was racing royalty, and I was always the lucky recipient of an invitation to an Indy 500 tradition: Mama Unser's annual barbecue.

Before Indianapolis had an NFL team franchise and before the Pacers became a competitive force in the NBA, the Indy 500 frenzy was equaled only by the famous "Sweet Sixteen" high school basketball tournaments that ended every basketball season. It's not difficult to understand high school basketball fever in Indiana once you see Gene Hackman's performance in the 1986 movie, *Hoosiers.* On the fifteenth anniversary of the 1954 Milan High School's state victory, many of the original team members appeared on one of our broadcasts, and the show received the highest ratings ever during its short life!

From high school basketball coaches to racecar drivers, we achieved a regional reputation as *the* local stage for visiting network personalities. Don Obermeyer of ABC Sports was a brilliant guest. Every May he would precede his production crew to do advance planning for the Indy 500 race. Don was funny and I loved his "inside" sports stories. But it all ended in 1975 when ABC-TV decided that the event was big enough for *Wide World of Sports* coverage, complete with TV vans, an expanded national crew, and much more coverage than could be provided by the local affiliate.

Jim McKay, the late ABC-TV sports anchor, was always a superb guest, chock-full of previously untold stories regarding famous athletes. Jim's finest hour was in 1972, when he solely anchored the coverage of the 1972 Munich Olympic Games massacre. To those of us who had worked with him it was not surprising to feel the humanity behind the coverage, as

Booking a broad range of guests for a local daytime talk show proved challenging and interesting.

he reported on one of the most horrendous episodes in the history of the Olympics.

On a much lighter side, and with much hype, we booked the first transvestite to "come out" of the closet: Christine Jorgenson. To put it mildly, it was tricky negotiating the minefield of viewer questions. While monitoring the final fifteen minute period of the show—when viewers called in their questions—I was able to connect only one out of every ten calls. In reality, very few of the viewer's questions could be aired on the public airwaves of the seventies. However, Christine was a wonderful sport and had a great sense of humor about her sex-change decision.

In fact, our local talk show would enjoy less than a year of airtime. Seems there was another local talk show in nearby Dayton, Ohio, that was achieving huge ratings. That show was the first to have a live studio audience, and the host roamed through the audience with a mike asking for audience participation. It was called *The Phil Donahue Show.*

Oh, well. Our show was given a proper funeral one rainy Friday morning when it was announced that *The Phil Donahue Show* would come to Indianapolis. Even as we were absorbing the shock, the studio curtains parted and in walked Phil Donahue himself! After a perfunctory round of applause, he made the appropriate comments and our crew left the building for much-needed drinks.

Phil Donahue quickly became a legend in broadcast TV. Starting at the local Dayton, Ohio, TV station, which shared ownership with the Indianapolis ABC-TV affiliate, Phil had a finger on the pulse of America. He instinctively understood that a new and different studio audience each day would add context to his guest's stories. Audience reactions would often guide the conversation between Phil and his guests. Interacting with the audience by roaming the studio with a hand-held mike created a different dynamic than simply interviewing a guest on a static set—the norm in the late 1970s. Today's TV talk show stars owe a huge debt of gratitude to the man who pioneered this format.

Although it was difficult for us to accept the loss of a locally based show, moving *The Phil Donahue Show* from Dayton to Indianapolis proved to be a ratings colossus for many decades.

Taking Action

I LOVED WORKING AT WLWI-TV AND was resolved to stay at the station even after the show's precipitous burial. While performing my duties for the talk show, I realized many viewers wrote to the station with a problem they needed solved. Knowing that the news anchors used this material for short segments when they required filler material, I proposed a new, regular ninety-second feature to station management that would be devoted to these letters: I called it *Action Line*, and lucky for me it was an instant hit!

Action Line became a regular feature on the 6 p.m. local news, and I was assigned the dual jobs of researching and writing each segment. I had obtained producer credits, but I would remain off-air; the news director wanted a newsperson to be the on-air talent. We would tape the following week's three segments every Friday afternoon, and this quickly became the highlight of my workweek.

That is, until David Letterman would saunter into the studio. David was the station's weekend weatherman and booth announcer. He was goofy; he was talented. He was also the most arrogant and opinionated person I had ever met. David loved to ridicule the reader letters and subsequent solutions provided by *Action Line*. He managed to see the dark side of the problems as a source for new jokes and comedy material. The more serious and offended I became, the more annoying (and funnier) he would become. One day I lost it and yelled, "Dave, get out of my studio and don't come back!" He did leave, laughing hysterically. And he didn't come back.

Years later, we managed to meet again. It was in the elevator of an apartment building on West 55th Street in Manhattan. I was with corporate ABC-TV and CBS had recently hired David to host its *Late Night Show*, after NBC replaced Johnny Carson with Jay Leno. David was waiting for construction on his Connecticut home to be completed and thus living in the city temporarily. When the elevator stopped at my floor, I asked David if he'd like to stop by for a drink. His memory of the seventies was intact. But although he *did* remind me that I'd once thrown him out of a TV studio, he graciously confined the rest of his comment to a simple "No, thanks" to the drink offer. It seemed that he had just finished walking a huge dog, so I was actually grateful for the reprieve.

The Next Jane Pauley?

B ACK IN THE INDIANAPOLIS DAYS, *Action Line* was rolling merrily along, but it hardly constituted the makings
of a career or a future. When I heard that Jane Pauley was
leaving the CBS-TV station in Indianapolis (literally across
the street from the ABC-TV affiliate where I worked) to become part of the NBC Chicago news team with Floyd Kal-
ber, I didn't hesitate to audition for the job.

First, I needed to take care of a few details: I dieted to
lose ten pounds, had porcelain veneers fitted for my front
teeth, and tried to refine my native New Jersey accent. There
were several dozen beautiful young women there for the audition. Many were recent graduates of Indiana University,
Jane Pauley's alma mater. I thought they were all terrific. I
knew that I was not.

Jane was just as caring and helpful in person as she later
presented herself on NBC's network morning show hit, *The
Today Show*. She kindly suggested to me that I leave my faux
hairpieces in the dressing room and skip the obviously fake
eyelashes. She tried, in vain, to help me soften my natural
East Coast accent.

It was clear that my audition competition fit her replacement role much better than I did. I made the first cut, but not the final cut. That's when I realized that that my on-air talent days were behind me.

The Indy 500: A Terrific Place for a Job Interview

"If you're not failing every now and again, it's a sign you're not doing anything very innovative."

Woody Allen

B Y THE MID-SEVENTIES, IT WAS clear that my television career was in a holding position, if not a stall. I still wrote and produced the news feature *Action Line* but my primary responsibilities had become secretarial, as administrative assistant to the station's program director. My title was Assistant Program Director, but my basic duties were typing and filing. Besides being underpaid and overworked, I now needed a career makeover.

It was a May weekend when I headed for the "time trials" that preceded the Indy 500 race each year. The VIP passes were pit passes, entitling the holder to enter a race driver's pit and meet the crew. Since my credentials were from the local ABC-TV station, I had a VIP pit pass. On a particular Sunday during the time trials weekend, I started a conversation with another "civilian" in the driver's pit. He was a very nice man who I quickly learned was the president of a large Midwest department store chain, L.S. Ayres & Company. The offices of the twelve-store division were based entirely in Indianapolis. When I asked why a modern multi-store chain in Indiana and Kentucky was still not advertising on television, he told me that his ad staff people were only familiar with newspaper and mail-order catalogs.

I must have been a fast talker because by the end of the day, I had created a new position for myself: Director of Broadcast Advertising for L.S. Ayres & Company. I started two weeks later at the grand salary of $15,000 a year.

The main advertising department of this twelve-store chain was comprised of a variety of people, most of whom had been there for a minimum of fifteen years. It was an amazing place. The copywriters sat in little four-by-five-foot cubicles. The copy chief showed up to work each day in a different funny hat, which she would wear all day. And the vice-president of the department played the piano in his office every day from 4:00 to 4:30 p.m.!

The place was certainly weird and archaic in many respects. Nevertheless, I saw something at the department store chain that I'd never before seen in the business world. I actually saw male vice-presidents and directors reporting to a woman and treating her with the utmost respect.

You Can Call Me Mrs. Rice

A s head of broadcast advertising, I would attend weekly merchandising meetings, even if they did not involve television or radio advertising, which most still did not. The most forward-thinking retailers still believed primarily in the power of print. The GMM, or general merchandise manager, who ran multiple departments consisting of several merchandise managers and buyers, headed up these weekly meetings.

Beverly Rice was a GMM, and the men who reported to her addressed her as Mrs. Rice. I was shocked at the respect she commanded: Remember, this was 1977. All the working women who I knew reported to men; men were the authority and women merely assisted them in their positions.

But Mrs. Rice was different. Her subordinate buyers would require her approval and confirmation over every major merchandise buy for their departments. She was definitive, fair, and knowledgeable in her decisions. I vowed that one day I would earn, and receive, that type of respect.

Mrs. Rice's weekly meetings were on par with attending a demanding class at a renowned business college. Preparing and summarizing each meeting was welcomed home-work, and although I was never awarded an MBA, I felt that I earned the equivalent of one. She was a diligent, no-non-sense professional who wielded and managed her power fairly, intuitively, and always to the best interest of the retail chain.

Mrs. Rice had started her career behind the cosmetics counter as a freelance "sales girl"—in mid-sixties parlance—performing makeup demonstrations each Saturday. She also worked with the fashion department, doing the makeup for the weekly fashion show models. She quickly mas-tered the business of fashion, understanding it from every standpoint: from the point of view of the fashion houses selling to the store buyers, to the consumer mind-set when shopping for clothes. I

> **I set new goals for myself. I would rise in my field. I would become an executive. I would be respected.**

saw firsthand the importance of knowing every detail of a business, yet having the ability to focus on the big picture. I learned how critical it is to build a trusted team where ev-eryone on the team is accountable.

Even more importantly, I learned how to make the diffi-cult decision to fire someone for incompetence or the inabil-ity to grow. These were the days before "downsizing" and often employees had to be terminated for non-performance. Mrs. Rice advised many times, "Phyllis, if that person is not going to be any better six months from now, then you should fire them today. You're actually doing them a favor and allowing them to move in a different direction. You are also being true to yourself and to those who pay you each week." A hard lesson, indeed, but it became my mantra in future years when faced with making the difficult decision to dismiss an employee and tasked with telling that employee that they were fired, and why.

"Co-op" money was the way department stores funded their ad campaigns, and I was fortunate when Mrs. Rice suggested that I accompany her to New York to help raise co-op dollars from major fashion houses for a fashion television campaign. She was respected in Indianapolis, but in New York Mrs. Rice was treated like a rock star. At the Seventh Avenue showrooms of the late seventies, I met all the major designers as they warmly greeted Mrs. Rice, kissing and hugging her: Bill Blass, Halston, Gloria Vanderbilt, and Diane von Furstenberg among others. Once again, I was welcomed into a new world in which an accomplished woman could achieve anything.

After the first New York trip, I set new goals for myself. I would study and learn from a woman like Beverly Rice. I would challenge myself to take advantage of every opportunity that came my way. And if one didn't come along, I would create it. I would rise in my field. I would become an executive. I would be respected.

Special Delivery

M E, DELIVER A SPEECH AT the New York Hilton to one
thousand people? Could I do this? The better question
was, "How could I *not* do this?"

Every January, the Television Bureau of Advertising, or
TVB, planned instructional seminars for their annual meeting at the N.Y. Hilton Hotel. Bear in mind that, back in the
seventies, television advertising was still in the dark ages.
However, there *were* success stories popping up across the
country, and the L.S. Ayres department store chain had
gained significant attention for its successes in using television to promote cosmetics, rugs, and furniture. Smart
retailers began to realize that this new medium—television—could help sell their products. The vice-president of
our department store (and my boss) would be presenting a
speech at this symposium, and I was drafted to prepare it.

Jim Rodefeld, who was vice-president of marketing for
the retail chain, was not entirely enthusiastic about traveling
to New York in a snowstorm. When I sensed his hesitation,
I volunteered to go instead and before he could change his

mind, I had packed up the slide show, made copies of my speech, and bought the plane tickets.

In later years Jim admitted that, had he known my appearance on that stage would lead to a new and better out-of-state job, he would have never approved my trip. But Jim was always a gentleman, and wished me every success.

I walked on stage at the N.Y. Hilton Hotel to address an audience of over one thousand. Little did I dream that sitting in the audience was the TV executive who would later call and offer me a job that changed my life.

Thirty days from the day I delivered the speech in the hotel's grand ballroom, I was on plane to Boston to meet with the general sales manager of WBZ-TV, New England's leading TV station. John Davison, the station's GSM, who had attended my seminar, afterward told me that he immediately called the president of Westinghouse Broadcasting and said, "I want that girl. I want her here to wake up those people at Filene's, Marshalls, and Bradlees, and get them to buy TV time from us...now!"

So began the odyssey of my Boston career.

Boston: The New Girl

FIRST IMPRESSIONS ARE CRUCIAL. THERE are always many details important to the first day at a new job. How long is the commute? What is the corporate culture like? What do I wear? How light or heavy on the makeup? Do I wear my shoulder-length hair flowing naturally or in a severe bun to look more "professional"?

Little did I realize that I would have a much more important issue to deal with on my first day of work at Boston's NBC affiliate, WBZ-TV. I arrived on the corporate campus promptly on what was supposed to be my first day at the job, only to hear the station was closed!

"How can a TV station be closed?" I asked the friendly guard. He told me the news department was at work, but the rest of the station was on a holiday.

"Don't you know it's Patriot's Day here in Boston, young lady? We're running the Boston Marathon today, and nobody has to work, unless they're essential."

Well, what were my choices?

I could not drive away quickly enough. Now that I felt

beyond stupid, I quickly sensed the "first day at work" adrenaline rush dissipate, and all concerns about first impressions totally evaporate. The next day, Tuesday, would now officially be my first day at my new job, at a new company, with new people everywhere. I braced for it.

Word had quickly spread that the new girl came to work on Patriot's Day, and everyone thought it was funny, at the expense of the new girl. I was embarrassed but determined to go along with their humor. Towards the end of my first day, a huge man appeared in my office doorway with a big smile on his face.

He introduced himself as Carl Yastrzemski, or "Yaz",

the renowned leading hitter of the Boston Red Sox. Yaz was scheduled for an interview with the sports anchor and he, also, heard that I had showed up for my first working day on Patriot's Day. The sports guys decided it would be really funny if Yaz came to my office to offer apologies on everyone's behalf for not having been told about Patriot's Day. Yaz was charming and his visit made my first day rather memorable.

Since the horrendous Boston Marathon bombing in 2013, Patriot's Day has attained a profoundly sad yet special meaning to everyone in the world. It is a tribute to the indomitable New England spirit that, despite this tragic episode, participants and spectators celebrate a bigger and better Boston Marathon every year.

Boston Is as Boston Does

I LOVED EVERYTHING ABOUT THE BOSTON area, from the sports teams to the change of seasons to the youthful college-town environment.

I learned to root for the Red Sox, because there *is* no other major league team in baseball. Well, not to a New England native, that is. But most of all, I found that the smart business people in the Boston area were receptive to innovation: amenable to fresh business models and to new people who could present original strategies and concepts in advertising and marketing to their customers.

My job title at WBZ-TV was retail sales manager, and my challenges were clear. The New England area was home to numerous retailers who had grown and expanded their businesses using traditional advertising techniques. Everyone I called upon had their *Boston Globe* ads tacked on their office walls. Television advertising was foreign terrain to them and they found it difficult, at first, to trust that a thirty-second commercial could bring a customer to their door the next day.

I felt like a pioneer in a strange territory with a dedicated mission. I needed a plan.

That's when I realized that I had a success story to tell. The big plus was that I spoke their language. I was able to translate the retail world of newspaper column inches into gross rating points and audience share of market. I charted an obstacle course with objectives and goals that would help lead WBZ-TV to the "Promised Land" of TV ad sales: the conversion of coveted advertising print dollars to television media budgets.

> I felt like a pioneer in a strange territory with a dedicated mission. I needed a plan.

I created the obstacle course, charted on one entire wall of my small office in the sales department. At the end of the course was the goal: a list of the who's who of retailers that had been household names in New England for decades, such as Jordan Marsh, Filene's, Marshalls, Bradlees, Stop & Shop, Star Markets, and more.

The obstacles were the hurdles of the traditional ad-buying mind-set and the difficulty of meeting and educating the retail GMMs and their ad people on the efficacy of TV advertising. Overcoming these obstacles meant meeting the decision-makers and proving to them there were many ways in which their customers made buying decisions. Today, with a myriad of digital and traditional media choices, it's hard to imagine that less than thirty years ago retailers still believed that print was their best—and in some cases, their only—way of effectively communicating with their consumers.

Progress developed faster than I ever imagined. With

my retail department store background, combined with the knowledge of TV ratings, costs, and content, the area's top retail executives welcomed and trusted me. One of my earliest converts was a young Harvard graduate who was part of the marketing team at Boston-based Star supermarkets. In later years he developed the concept of retail stores catering to small and large businesses with equipment and supplies. His concept evolved from a few Boston-area outlets to the international chain that later became known as Staples. To this day, I look forward to Tom Stemberg's annual holiday newsletters. Tom was, and is, a true visionary.

Life was good. My daily Mass Pike commute from Wellesley to Boston was a pleasure. Every Friday afternoon I met with John Davison, our general sales manager, to recount my latest accomplishments and absorb his constructive feedback. Then late one Friday afternoon, I answered my office phone and spoke with a man who would help write the next chapter of my career.

Build More Than a Career: Build a Brand

OVER THE YEARS I HAD worked hard at many aspects of building a career, not the least of which was developing the art of self-promotion. Today we call it "building your brand." Far too often, it's later in life when many talented men and women learn the difficult lesson that they did not take the necessary steps to brand themselves early in their career path. Each of us has a unique set of skills. Marketing those skills through self-promotion can help propel a career. This is not a self-serving act; it is professional survival.

I volunteered to mentor a group of students at a local Boston college, Fisher College, introducing these students to the everyday realities of the actual business world. Since my business world was a television station, my group became extremely popular.

During the second year of this program, I accepted the honor of delivering the commencement address at the June graduation ceremony of Fisher College. I thought, "No big deal; just 250 graduates." What I failed to realize was that each graduate invites up to eight relatives and friends to attend their graduation. Since the ceremony would take place at downtown Boston's John Hancock Auditorium, this should have been a red flag to indicate I would be addressing almost two thousand people! It was the New York Hilton all over again.

As I walked in the processional leading to the stage, I focused on the speech. I hoped my words were meaningful and tried to concentrate on the 250 graduates who would now be leaving their comfortable college cocoon and embarking on a new life.

The positive press that followed this commencement speech complemented my business accomplishments that had begun to accumulate. As word spread of the success that this Boston television station was experiencing in penetrating the advertising budgets of the retail world, so did my reputation. Westinghouse Broadcasting, the owners of WBZ-TV, had been among the first to recognize the void of retail advertising when they created my position. Soon to follow were the major networks, all located in that mecca of advertising: New York City.

ABC-TV was at the forefront of the network's search for retail marketing managers. The difficulty was finding those executives who could comfortably straddle the world of TV media and the retail mindset. As a former retailer who made the transition to television, I knew I was the right person in the right place at the right time.

Yet, the reality was that even with my Boston successes, the two critical factors that landed me in the Big Apple were self-promotion and building my brand. I encourage every man and woman in the working world today to think of themselves as a product: a product with specific skills, aptitudes, knowledge, and a track record. Marketability is the key to advancement and change in the span of a career and often the tipping point of why you got the callback and landed the job.

The same advice applies to every business owner. Despite adversity and setbacks, never give up. As Jimmy Valvano, the famed basketball coach, who left the world far too young, always said, "Never, ever give up."

Flying the Friendly Skies?

M ANY POSITIVE FACTORS LED TO my career move to New York City. But the move also fostered many challenges, some more subtle than others. In addition to the other difficulties faced in my first few months in New York, I was still commuting weekly to my home in Wellesley, a suburb of Boston. I was a Monday morning/Friday evening commuter on the former Eastern Air Lines that flew a daily shuttle plane between Boston and New York. I had rented a small studio apartment that served as my weekday home, and spent weekends with my family whenever I could.

Was it difficult to start a new job in a new company, and then spend each night in an empty apartment? Of course it was. But the lesson learned was that if you want to advance in your chosen career, be prepared to make sacrifices and change your lifestyle. Personal comfort and a professional safe haven can lead to a stagnant career. Don't be afraid to reach for the brass ring. Most people have opportunities in their career life, but unfortunately, only a few recognize when to jump in and move on.

I quickly adjusted to the perils and the positives of this

weekly commute. I learned never to let your seatmate start a conversation because it may not end until the plane lands. Exchange a few pleasantries, and then open a book or a spreadsheet. I learned that I could adapt to waking at 4:00 a.m. every Monday morning to catch the 7:00 a.m. flight at Logan Airport. I learned the meaning of "quality time" spent with family.

Accepting this promotion to ABC Network was the most important step I could take to further my career; I had worked and trained hard for this. Furthermore, by being in the right place at the right time I had landed in the number one TV market in the country! And I was pleasantly surprised when the editor of the Eastern Air Lines monthly magazine chose to showcase my "dual career marriage" with a splashy profile presenting my career choice, my family, and of course, my weekly commute.

My husband and I had jointly decided that for the next six months he would interview for a media job in New York. If he were unsuccessful, I would most likely move back to Boston. His radio credentials were solid and the NBC Radio Network hired him shortly thereafter. My two sons, Robert and Steven, were in college, and my daughter, Suzanne, became a senior-year boarding student at Dana Hall Prep School. I was on my way up. I was ready for prime time.

No Office, No Desk, No Problem!

I MAY HAVE FELT READY FOR prime time, but the New York prime time scene was not yet ready for me. I knew I was at the proverbial right place at the right time, and I was convinced my timing could not be better. Yet the first few weeks at WABC-TV were the most difficult and challenging that I would ever endure in my career. And, I would add, the most humiliating.

I started my first day on the job on a high note, running up the steps of Burlington House on Avenue of the Americas: I felt like Mary Tyler Moore! Fans of the vintage seventies sitcom series will remember that Mary worked at a TV station in Minneapolis. The opening shot of the show features Mary running through the downtown streets, throwing her hat in the air, the gesture joyfully implying, "Here I am, ready to go to work!"

My premature enthusiasm was completely diminished when I learned that the general sales manager of WABC-TV, to whom I reported, was completely surprised when I showed up at his door. Not only had he forgotten about my start date, but there was no office, no cubicle, and no chair available for me that first day.

After a few hours of wishing I were back in my formative Boston days, the manager told me I could temporarily occupy the small office of a research director who was on vacation. The following week I was shuffled to another office of a vacationing staff person. Finally, I was told that I could use the conference room as an office with the provision that I had to leave whenever the room was booked for a meeting. I began working with a portable file crate, my old Rolodex, and the conference room telephone. This was the 80s, so no cell phones and no computer unless you were using it for sales inventory. It was humiliating to look up and see eight or so men walking into the conference room for their meeting with the expectation that I would immediately leave. I played the good soldier and did as I was told.

> I began working with a portable file crate, my old Rolodex, and the conference room telephone.

The clincher was that the executive who had actually interviewed and hired me had resigned the week prior, to return to his former retail position, far away from the politics and lack of respect he experienced in his brief six months at ABC.

Bob Gottleib had been a New York department store vice-president of marketing. ABC employed him to spearhead the hiring of retail sales managers like me, who could bridge the communication gap between TV sales and the retail world.

Therefore, the only person I knew and trusted was no longer at the network. Seasoned male sales pros viewed me with suspicion. Experienced female assistants resented my title and responsibilities. Feeling alone in this strange world was difficult, but even more difficult was the estrangement I experienced from the rest of the staff.

Welcome to the Alpha Boys Club

JUMPING FROM THE WORLD OF upscale retail in Indianapolis to the world of media at Boston's WBZ television station had not been a difficult transition. Both working environments had recognized and rewarded talent and ambition among either sex. However, nothing would prepare me for the sexual undercurrents I would endure as the first female sales manager of the country's number one television station, the flagship New York station of ABC-TV.

"What's that girl doing here anyway?"

"She never worked anywhere at ABC so how come she's a sales manager?"

"We don't need a girl wanting to hang out with us when we go drinking."

"I'm not letting her anywhere near my clients!"

"I hear she's Jewish, not Irish like most of us."

The Alpha Boys Club was unaccustomed to working with a woman on a level playing field. Many managers throughout the Owned Station Division had helped achieve their positions by their willingness to relocate their families around the country, greatly assisting their climb to the top. To a man, I was the outsider who hadn't paid her dues. On top of that, I was a woman, crashing into their formerly male-dominated bastion of power.

I endured their off-color jokes every day. I was the target of specific references to my anatomy. The vice-president of sales, to whom I reported, asked me to take off my bra during an airplane trip to a national sales managers meeting! Today, it would take mere minutes to file a lawsuit for sexual harassment. Thirty years ago, such action could have quickly ended my career.

The semi-annual meetings of all sales managers from the ABC-TV Owned Station Division always presented an unwelcome and new set of challenges. After the perfunctory two-hour morning business meetings, the afternoons were devoted to sports competition. Hard to believe that just thirty years ago, dominance of a daily macho-styled sports agenda served to reaffirm a sales manager's reputation and greatly enhance his future opportunities for promotion. There were tugs-of-war, sprint races, beach volleyball, and basketball events. Sounds like a lot of fun, unless you are the only woman involved. I was often given a striped referee shirt, a clipboard, and a scorecard. What else could they do with me?

I played the "good sport" while always feeling the pervasive disconnect from the group, and learned to endure the long days of sports activities and "bonding" dinners to which I was seldom invited.

My last year at ABC I was finally joined by a second woman manager, from station WXYZ-TV, Detroit. Barbara was a slight woman with a well-deserved reputation for her sales skills and marketing accomplishments. She built an advertising agency that carried her name and, in later years after ABC, she solidified her marketing credibility by bringing the Martha Stewart brand to K-Mart for breakthrough product lines and endorsements. I felt fortunate to have Barbara at my side, although she, too, felt helpless to cope with the overt sexual harassment we experienced.

The most egregious episode happened at a February sales managers' meeting, just prior to the short morning business presentation. It's fairly common to show brief videos prior to the start of business. They're called "ice-breakers" because they help attendees to focus on the screen, perhaps chuckle or laugh and appreciate the action. When the audience is focused, initiating the business agenda becomes easier. Well, this "ice-breaker" video was off the charts! It consisted of ten minutes of Asian women displaying their pubic hairs while being shaved and dyed to various colors—even red, white, and blue.

Nothing was left to the imagination. "Barbara, we should walk right out of this dark conference room. This is pornographic and obscene," I whispered. She felt conflicted and whispered back that it would be over in minutes and our absence would be obvious. "It'll give them one more reason to feel that we don't fit in," she added. So my insecurities overruled my intellect and I stayed. I was more concerned with being deemed a sophisticated businesswoman rather than a squeamish girl. To this day, I wish I had left my seat and slammed the door behind me. But in later years I remembered the sensible saying: "What doesn't kill you will make you stronger." And it did.

I wasn't in any danger of being killed and while my sensitivities were damaged, they eventually healed. Yet this incident left me more determined than ever to prove I belonged, if only to myself. Little did I realize that every insult and unpleasant episode I experienced during my six-year ABC-TV career would magnify my resolve to always be accountable to myself and no one else.

Gottlieb had realized, quite early, that he would never be accepted by this sales group and up and left. I, however, was determined to prove my worth by parlaying my Boston market successes to New York City retailers. I gave myself six months to make my first score and targeted the biggest retailer in the city: Macy's. At that time, the retailer would consistently buy fifteen to twenty newspaper pages per week. I dreamt of converting a share of those huge retail ad budgets to television time.

The ABC-TV network, with its spectacular midtown office building, had six private dining rooms on its penthouse floor. Corporate executives from General Motors, Kraft Foods, Proctor and Gamble, and hundreds of other valued advertisers were wined and dined in these private and privileged dining rooms. Hard to believe, but no retail president or senior executive had ever set foot in the thirty-sixth-floor dining venue. This would quickly change when I realized what a great opportunity the venue provided to showcase our media plans in an impressive, private setting. Of course, if by any chance, Barbara Walters or Frank Gifford or Howard Cosell stopped by to say hello, well, that would be the icing on the sales cake! I convinced my general sales manager and sales colleagues that by developing a targeted executive invitee list of every major department store, supermarket chain, and specialty chain, we would be way ahead of NBC and CBS in our retail sales endeavors.

As luck would have it, the then-president of ABC-TV network, Leonard Goldenson, visited my first retail lunch and introduced himself to Marvin Traub, CEO of Bloomingdale's. Both men were impressed with each other! We then arranged weekly "retail lunches" and soon the network dining rooms became a glamorous show-business-type midday retreat for top marketing executives throughout the tri-state area. I became a very popular hostess, even when my hidden agenda became obvious to all.

I learned that often your best-selling tools are literally under your nose. Don't be intimated by precedent and don't be afraid to carve out some new rules.

I traveled around the country to retail trade shows so I could spend valuable time with key retailers, closing my first TV co-op money deal at the Chicago Housewares Show at McCormick Place. The big furniture trade show in North Carolina was a perennial on my list as was the Las Vegas Electronics show. My time consisted of lots of unglamorous travel and boring dinners, but my actions helped build a reputation that "TV people" understood the retail business and could help move their merchandise.

As I forged valuable relationships with marketing executives at Macy's, Bloomingdale's, and Saks Fifth Avenue, I slowly helped evolve their marketing plans to automatically include broadcast advertising. Just as slowly, I began to experience a measure of trust and respect from my peers.

Sales people respect sales. There is nothing like "new

money" to make a manager smile. Joe Ahern, a tough Philadelphia-born general sales manager, was among the first to see that my gender, my religion, and my lack of paying dues from within the ABC-TV corporate ladder were all irrelevant to his bottom line. His enthusiasm and encouragement helped me sleep better at night in those first months. I still wasn't invited to happy hour drinks with the boys, but that no longer mattered.

Staying focused and staying tough during those New York years helped build my resolve and taught me sales lessons that were critical in dealing with people and building a new business in later years. "Whatever it takes" was the sales mantra in New York, and I learned that the foremost rule in making the sale was first to be likable and humble. Simply stated, people do business with people whose company they enjoy, so it's important to always create ways to make it easy to foster a relationship. Commu-

There are certain realities you always have to face: your product and/or your services are not unique.

nicate with your customer or client. Be the first to know if they're unhappy or considering a change. There are certain realities you always have to face: your product and/or your services are not unique. There is always stellar competition. Nonetheless, people do business with people they like. That lesson was embedded in my soul.

Years later, as I built the business model and developed the culture at Green Advertising, I knew how important the likability factor was. A dose of humility never hurt, along with the knowledge that we were problem-solvers in a highly competitive environment. To this day I remind our staff that clients have many choices and, on a given day, they may not be 100 percent happy with our creativity or the account management. But if you've built a reservoir of trust and comfort within the relationship, minor blips along the road will be quickly resolved.

I realized in later years that the myriad of challenges and roadblocks I had faced in those early network days served to strengthen my belief in my capabilities and fortify trust in my expertise when it was time to take a new step into the unchartered waters of entrepreneurship in Florida. The old Frank Sinatra song about New York states, "If I can make it there, I'll make it anywhere!"

This proved to be the catalyst for my future entrepreneurial life.

Barbara Walters Was So Nice to Me; Howard Cosell, Not So Much

UPON PROMOTION TO DIRECTOR OF retail marketing, I needed a good professional photo to accompany the initial publicity releases sent to the press. I arrived early for my appointment with one of the network photographers and was directed to take a seat in the "makeup room." I gladly took the most convenient chair but in my rush failed to see a card that read "Barbara Walters" attached to it. I *did* notice that there were some random items on the chair that I carefully placed on the floor.

About ten minutes after the photography session started, the door opened and Barbara Walters entered. As the first female news anchor in television, she was my number one idol. I knew that she had endured years of prejudice from male network executives who maintained that only men would command the authority to deliver the nightly news. Barbara evolved from her news position to maintain a commanding TV presence as she changed the interview style of television forever.

After a few awkward minutes, Barbara sweetly asked

about the location of her attaché case and jacket. I was mortified! I mumbled an apology as I knelt on the floor to retrieve her possessions. Barbara just laughed as she congratulated me. She looked at me very sincerely and gave me some quite valuable tips for portrait photography. She was charming and lovely.

Then there was Howard Cosell.

I would encounter the formidable Howard en route to the private dining rooms of the network. The operative word here is "private."

The first time I saw him, he stared at me and asked, "Where do you think you're going, little lady?"

As I punched the elevator button for the thirty-sixth floor, I stared back at the big, hulking man who asked me this question. Suffice to say he was tall and intimidating and although I proceeded to my lunch, it was quite unnerving. I later learned that Howard Cosell talked to everyone in the same voice. His non-broadcast voice was always condescending; his colleagues were accustomed to it. I could never say that Howard became a friend, but his terse greetings quickly ceased to feel threatening.

Creating the First Infomercial

ONE OF THE FIRST AREAS I wanted to tackle in my new position was developing a unique format to attract advertisers to television in the competitive New York media market. The team and I developed a one-minute infomercial concept featuring well-known magazine editors. The concept was simple: create an environment for the advertiser that gives the commercial announcement additional credibility. In today's social media parlance this is labeled "content advertising."

The first major magazine editor who saw the value in promoting the magazine brand was Marshall Loeb, the editor of *Money Magazine,* published by Time, Inc. It was pretty heady stuff to walk into the Time/Life building on Avenue of the Americas with a TV crew each month. A small ABC-TV minicam crew would shoot thirty-second vignettes in Mr. Loeb's office. A client, such as a major bank, would buy sixty seconds of TV time: thirty seconds of *Money Magazine* tips, married to a thirty-second commercial, hence creating a favorable environment for the advertising message. This was long before the days of the two-minute infomercial, or the thirty-minute infomercial program, so it was a fresh, new concept and one that quickly grew marketing legs and attracted such corporate giants as American Express.

ABC would promote *Money Magazine's* financial tips in the first thirty seconds, and the paid commercial would follow. We cleverly named this concept an "infomercial"!

A year after ABC-TV had approved the infomercial concept, and with the *Money Magazine* success behind us, we proceeded to develop *Fashion Tips* featuring Dorothy Kalins, then-editor of *Metropolitan Home Magazine*, published by Meredith Publications. Gimbels New York sponsored this fashion infomercial. Word of the new TV concept by ABC had spread throughout the publishing world and soon I had appointments with John Mack Carter, editorial guru of *Good Housekeeping* and Helen Gurley Brown, the original *Cosmo Girl* and respected author.

I was so close to this original concept that I failed to see the broader implications and revenue possibilities of the sixty-second infomercial. With well-known and extremely competent print editors clamoring for this new form of exposure, the copywriting and syndication possibilities of the innovative revenue stream were almost limitless. Today, as an entrepreneur, I would move mountains to retain recognizable magazine editors to long-term contracts as spokespeople for their various niche markets of finance, fashion, and furnishings. Of course, the concept now thrives within the context of social media in various forms of content marketing and has become a staple of the social media marketing paradigm.

But the world was a little more simplistic in the mid-

1980s. While working at the New York flagship station, WABC-TV, I convinced Joe Ahern, the general sales manager, of the incremental revenue this concept would and actually did deliver. Yet when promoted to ABC-TV Owned Stations division, the heavy hand of bureaucracy and turf warfare brought the expansion of the concept to a quick standstill. Camera people and directors were far removed from the sales staff. TV editors were another step removed, all mired in the tradition of "separation of church and state." Negotiating the minefields of inter-departmental network politics became insurmountable. To the sales executives of the network and the Owned-Station division, the innovative concept was small potatoes, and it was not worth creating a divisive relationship to pursue it.

The Original Cosmo Girl

WHEN YOUR TEENAGE IDOL WALKS into your office, it is a memorable day. Upon entering my formative teenage years, Helen Gurley Brown's famous groundbreaking book, *Sex and the Single Girl*, was every girl's bible. Helen's descriptions and approval of unmarried sex were a breath of fresh air in a world of teenage angst, insecurity, and self-consciousness. I knew that Helen was in her seventies so I didn't quite know what to expect that day; I should have known that she would still project the essence of "the Cosmo gal."

She looked amazing, adorned with fishnet stockings, stiletto heels, a form-hugging black knit dress, casual scarf, and glittering costume jewelry. To complete her signature look, her "mod" makeup was set off by the longest faux eyelashes I had ever seen! She was funny, direct, saucy, and totally prepared with sample scripts. We talked for hours, and if I had the final word, I would have signed her up that day.

A week later, I was *totally* blindsided by my boss's refusal to offer Helen a contract proposal for a series of "Cosmo Tips." The two executives to whom I reported felt that she was too old to be marketable and that it would be difficult to secure an "advertorial" sponsor. My rebuttals were all dismissed. I insisted that she looked like most women in their forties and that her reputation, humor, and wit would resonate with the TV audiences. My boss totally missed the boat on this one. Interestingly, Hearst Corporation kept Ms. Brown involved in their publishing empire for another twenty years! She always had her fingers on the pulse of today's woman, regardless of the era.

Five Things I Learned from My Cosmo Girl Experience

1. Age is only a number and should not be a defining barrier; knowledge, expertise, and reputation are more realistic benchmarks when determining the marketability of a personality. The TV networks learned that lesson when they played musical chairs in their mission to appoint network news anchors.

2. Fight for what you believe. I gave up after the first try. Be confident even when your ideas are not immediately recognized. I learned that often it takes five *nos* before you get a *yes* to a new concept.

3. Stay in shape and look great for as long as you can: perception is reality. People who look good are judged as more competent and smarter all the time.

4. If you want to be recognized as a leader, then don't be afraid to lead. Be persistent and courageous, even if your ideas seem unpopular at the time.

5. Stay connected. After my "Cosmo" concept was rejected, I never connected with HGB again. Big mistake. She remained a popular and respected personality in the publishing business, and the wife of movie mogul David Brown. I learned in later years that "connections are magic." Don't waste the opportunity.

We never went forward with "Cosmo Tips" although I knew it could be a winner. Some of her commentary might push the envelope but women would relate to her, just as I did as a young teenager about to enter the curious and confusing world of teenage boys.

Part Two

———

THE SHAKE-UP

Outplacement: My First Step to Becoming an Entrepreneur

"Change is the law of life. And those who look only to the past or present are certain to miss the future."

John F. Kennedy

T HE CONCEPT OF OUTPLACEMENT SERVICES sounds nurturing and comforting. The reality is quite different. Large corporations have adopted a business model whereby newly fired employees are given temporary office accommodations to help them transition from a corporate title and weekly paycheck to a new working environment. But instead of feeling nurtured in a small cubicle on a strange floor at ABC-TV, I felt alone, awkward, and stripped of my identity. I was allowed to occupy this sterile cubicle for six weeks and avail myself of the many office services to which I had become accustomed.

Although I'd been fired, I was determined to make the temporary office situation work to my advantage. I still had the network address and telephone at my disposal and the outside world was unaware and unconcerned about my

> **Although I'd been fired, I was determined to make the temporary office situation work to my advantage.**

present job status. I remembered that often the best opportunities are literally under your nose. My mission was to quickly find freelance jobs that would supplement my meager unemployment compensation checks, while I sorted out my options and decided whether to stay in New York City or to move elsewhere in the country.

Though times were uncertain and difficult, there was an upside: I had no idea how many interesting people I would meet and work with during this initial foray outside the world of corporate America. The first classified ad that I answered led to an interview at the office of world-renowned artist Paul Simon. As I walked into that famous landmark, the Brill Building on Broadway, I recognized that I needed to seriously "sell" myself as the answer to whatever problems I would potentially hear. My successful interview with Eddy Simon, Paul's brother, led to a part-time position as national sales manager for a small Hampton Bays radio station owned by Eddy Simon, Lorne Michaels, and Paul Simon.

Eddy had explained that the salespeople at the station had no problem attracting local advertisers, particularly in the summer months. What the station needed were advertisers such as supermarket chains and retailers that would air promotions year-round. Their major objective was selling airtime to large retailers located in Suffolk County, New

York, but with management offices in metropolitan New York and New Jersey.

This was a perfect fit for me. I was on a first-name basis with many media decision-makers at large food chains, department stores, and specialty chains. I knew how to develop co-op programs, promotions, and special events. I built a trusting relationship with the famous station owners and delivered new revenue and business opportunities to this small gem of a radio station.

Not surprisingly, the perk I most enjoyed from this job was attending *Saturday Night Live* shows in Manhattan as Lorne Michael's guest and meeting the famous hosts and stars. This was the era when John Belushi, Dan Aykroyd, Gilda Radner, and Eddie Murphy were among the show's legendary luminaries. Meeting these famous people in person was a weekly "high" for me.

Too bad it was only temporary!

Choose Something You Love to Do

It's said that if you find a job you love and work with people you like, you'll never really work another day in your life. That's not really true. There are always good days and bad days. Good talent often goes unrecognized. Good presentations are ignored. Deserving people do not get the promised promotion.

One of the most difficult decisions you'll ever make is whether to go in pursuit of the "right" job after you've been let go. Or should you instead take a deep breath, look at your bank account, and plot a course to self-ownership?

The biggest problem for most people is that they wait too long to make either decision. The "loser" emotions caused by unemployment result in a never-ending, downward spiral of feelings of defeat and despair. Then the doubts creep in. Will I ever be employed again? What if I start my own business and fail? Can I adjust to the lack of a weekly payroll check?

Taking the step to entrepreneurship may not be for everyone. But the first stride in the right direction after being fired is to take responsibility for what happened to you. The day I was fired was the day I felt victimized. ABC-TV was acquired by a lean, bottom-line focused company where trimming the payroll was the number one priority. I told myself and everyone who would listen that I was an early victim of their turnaround plan. "Look at my new business track record. Note the major retail accounts on the network's sales computers for which I am personally responsible," I'd tell myself. I blamed Cap Cities executives, ABC's top tier sales team, and even some of my colleagues.

Another marketing person, Molly, who shared my outplacement office, served as a good sounding board for me. The first week in our new quarters she cried every day. I would tell her, "Molly, you're only thirty-two. You have so many good working years ahead. Look at me, a fifty-year-old who worked my way up, only to be blindsided by my new bosses." The more she cried, the more I talked.

One day I had an epiphany. Maybe *I* was responsible for not evolving to a position considered vital and important to the new owner's business strategy. Perhaps I was so focused on the success story—starring me—that I failed to include and nurture colleague relationships. To the outside world, I was a successful marketing executive and salesperson, raking in new retail revenue. To our internal company, I was perceived as a loner, gaining recognition, but not genuine admiration.

Analyzing the career I carefully crafted at ABC-TV, I realized although I was successful in the retail sales niche, I never expanded my skills and talent to forge relationships with the other major corporations who were placing millions and billions of their media budgets into TV. I was content to develop co-op advertising plans for Macy's and Bloomingdale's, with major bedding manufacturers, appliance companies, and furniture manufacturing heavyweights. I was in my comfort zone with the knowledge that each year's media budgets continued to head upwards.

I did have a lot of success stories. Being responsible for new retail dollars pouring into our network programming, I convinced my bosses to help fund a breakthrough consumer shopping study. This was a true New York City first! With the advice and help of Dick Bruskin, owner of the Bruskin Study, we convinced the eight major New York/New Jersey area department stores to financially participate in the research study analyzing consumer's attitudes and shopping behavior.

The informational results were interesting, but the key accomplishment was the creation of a trusting relationship between the TV networks and the retailers. This bond showed that the networks were genuinely sincere in their pursuit of retailer media dollars. ABC-TV paid for half of the study; the balance was funded through participation by all the major retailers.

In hindsight, I should have reached beyond the retail world, to the marketing departments of companies such as Sony, Sealy, American Express, and others. I had the knowledge and talent to speak "marketing language" as opposed to media talk. This strategy had achieved significant results with every major retailer in my book. Why didn't I expand this strategy to play a larger role in new business development? I was dealing with budgets under $1 million, when I should have set my sights higher, to talk to the big boys with their $100 million-plus media budgets.

The Quickest Path to a New Career

1. Get over the bitterness and anger. It's destructive.

2. Don't wait too long to move forward. You may not feel ready for that new interview and may dread being asked, "Why did you leave your last job?" Remember, the best answer is the right answer. Take responsibility for what happened and talk about what you learned. There's no shame in being fired. Put the spotlight on the real cause for your termination. Be authentic.

3. Make a decision. This may seems obvious, but it's hard. How can you feel good about working for half of your previous salary? How can you feel good about reporting to someone twenty years younger? You're never 100 percent sure, but convince yourself to take the shot.

4. Is this the right time to fulfill your burning desire to become your own boss? If so, get your ducks in order. It may sound obvious to conduct an initial research of the competitive landscape before taking the plunge, but many would-be entrepreneurs look first to their accountant and then to their lawyer. Perhaps take a part-time or freelance job to keep the cash flow while you're planning your new venture.

5. Keep the network channels open. You've spent years building your personal network, starting with your high school and college classmates. The list has multiplied with each new job, with every vendor you've hired, with old and new acquaintances. Your days may be filled with more questions than you can answer. Continual social networking takes effort: It's time well invested.

After a few years, as retailers became more comfortable in planning broadcast as a vital allocation in their advertising budgets, my pioneer role grew diminished. I had opened the doors to a significant new revenue stream; now the sales pros would fight for their share of the media pie. Additionally, I didn't have too many trusted friends in the company. I hadn't cultivated any mentors. It was not difficult for the new owners to eliminate my position. There was little fall-out. They made astute business decisions, and this one affected me.

Only when I finally took ownership and responsibility for losing my job was I able to focus clearly on a path leading to realism and optimism. I learned the first step to a new career move, whether it's a job or starting your own business, is to stop blaming others for what's happened to you. You have the same skills and knowledge you had the day before you were fired. Now it's time to go to work in a new direction.

Don't Waste Time

L ET'S GO BACK TO THE second point in the previous chapter: "Don't Wait Too Long." This is the biggest mistake made today by previously employed workers.

With the 2008-2009 recession causing employers across the country to lay off hundreds of thousands of workers a month and an unemployment rate reaching double digits, many industry jobs never returned. Getting rehired in another industry proved to be even more difficult for those who had not been employed for six months or longer. Several studies at the time showed that the state of being unemployed by itself had become a sorting criterion, and that being unemployed for more than ten months decreased interview requests by 20 percent overall.

According to a *New York Times* article published late in 2013, "New evidence shows that bias plays a much larger role than previously thought. Some of the long-term unemployed might never find work because businesses refuse to hire them. Some fear that long-term joblessness has permanently scarred the American work force, knocking the economy off its long-term growth trend."

When you lose your job and become a statistic it's not easy to wake up the next morning and deal with reality. But this is exactly what you need to do. Your new job is simply *finding a job*.

Sure, the termination package or severance pay will help ease the pain. The months of unemployment compensation may even pay most of the bills. You're nursing a lot of pain and may feel like a loner, or even worse, a loser.

> **When the unemployment checks stopped, the fear of failing kicked in. I forced myself to find a full-time job at one-third of my previous salary.**

I know the feeling. Everyone looked busy and successful in the months I walked the streets of New York City after losing my job. Everybody looked in a hurry to get somewhere. I was juggling freelance jobs between weekly trips to the unemployment office. Searching only for jobs in the broadcast industry was a mistake. In hindsight, the best move would have been to look outside my limited industry. I knew how to "make the sale." I had terrific presentation skills. I should have been open and willing to start anew, maybe in another industry; perhaps with a pay cut, but I'd be working full-time.

When the unemployment checks eventually stopped, the fear of failing kicked in. I forced myself to find a full-time job at one-third of my previous salary. But guess what, I was working! Now read about my Barter Advantage experience.

From the Four Seasons to Tuna Fish

B ARTER ADVANTAGE WAS A COMPANY that proved to be a huge stepping stone to learning creative ways to run a profitable business. Barter Advantage was located way uptown on Third Avenue in a high-rise office building. Their revenue was derived from paying members who bartered their services to other members on an as-need basis. Profitability was difficult in the barter business, so the owner decided that an in-house advertising agency could be a new revenue source, attracting new members with this additional capability.

I proceeded to sell myself again. I convinced the owner that, with my media expertise, I could easily develop the structure and implementation of an on-site advertising agency. Wow! Easier said than done, but I was hired. I soon discovered how little I actually knew.

OK. I knew how to sell. But what did I know about starting and building an advertising agency? I needed hands-on

experience. I needed to learn more about the business side of the advertising business.

From my office, a six-by-six cubicle, I worked twelve hours a day trying to learn the business of a start-up in-house advertising firm. Everyone ordered tuna sandwiches for lunch, and so did I. This was a long way from the expense-account lunches at the Four Seasons and Smith & Wollensky, but it was an incredible learning experience for me.

So while I juggled meetings with large advertisers to bring revenue to the Simon's radio station, I arranged meetings with many friends who worked with ad firms. I quickly learned that the agency side is a world apart from network sales. With an urgency to have this new ad firm up and running, I quickly learned the basic rules of billing, fees, and deadlines. Becoming knowledgeable about the business objectives of many barter members was critical, so that I could advise them on media placement and also write and create their ad campaigns. I never thought that my two-decade-old copywriting experience would be as useful as it turned out to be in the year I spent at Barter Advantage!

More importantly, I observed and absorbed the daily rigors of seeing an entrepreneur work in a less-than-glamorous business. The owner, a fortyish single woman, had built the business from the bottom up. I respected and admired her stamina in maintaining constant twelve-hour days and her dedication to her clients, yet with one eye always on the bottom line. Lois, the owner, proved to be a true female role model with whom I could identify, and hopefully emulate in the future.

After a soul-searching year, post the corporate ABC-TV world, I realized that my destiny was not to juggle freelance jobs and continually search for new opportunities, but to face the reality that I needed to consider difficult decisions and take on new challenges in order to achieve true financial security. Many may think people make major tough decisions in their lives due to the inspiration or influence of others. For me, the most important lifetime decision I would ever make was born of fear: the sheer fear of becoming penniless as I became older, the fear of being fired once again, the fear of having no control over the rest of my life.

Out of desperation tinged with fear, I knew I would have to make a life-altering decision. I had little to lose and perhaps a promising future to gain. The year was 1986. If any fortune-teller had predicted that twenty-five years later I would be so financially secure, I would never have believed it. If I had been told that twenty-five years later I would achieve all my dreams, I would have laughed...or cried. Through time I found the old saying, "The harder you work the luckier you are," contains more than a grain of truth.

Shake It Up!

TURNING FIFTY AND LOSING MY recognizable career and identity was terrifying. I had been raised in a generation of women in which the role model of Doris Day had evolved into the teachings of Gloria Steinem. As the noted author Erica Jong wrote in her book *Fear of Fifty*, "Fifty is the time when time itself seems short." So here I was at the crossroads of my life at fifty, and remembered the George Gordon Byron (Lord Byron) poem from *Don Juan*:

> When people say, "I've told you *fifty* times,"
> They mean to scold, and very often do:
> When poets say, "I've written fifty rhymes,"
> They make you dread that you'll recite them too;
> In gangs of *fifty*, thieves commit their crimes;
> At *fifty* love for love is rare, 'tis true,
> But then, no doubt, it equally as true is,
> A good deal may be bought for *fifty* Louis.

So why was all this happening to me at fifty? Did I really have my best years ahead? After my initial trepidation, I was determined to jump in and find out. I call it "shaking up your life," and I encourage others to do so. Many people feel they cannot move, relocate, and reinvent themselves. They have spouses and other responsibilities that bind them to live in their present situation. But even to those who are convinced that they could never move away from their friends and families, losing a job can be the best wake-up call they'll ever get to bring about positive change.

An unemployed person awakes each morning with a sense of emptiness caused by the disappearance of a normal working routine. A person without a specific place to go each morning, whether an office, a factory, or a retail store, often feels helpless and out-of-touch with the rest of the world.

I know, because I walked this path. Your friends and families are usually terrific support systems, but recognize that they are delivering only external support. What you need is internal support. And only you can develop the core of inner strength by digging deep into the "who" of you, not the "what." Do you have to stay in that apartment or home? Can you continue your career and find a decent job somewhere else in the country? Can you seek employment in another industry in another city? To many, even the thought of such change is scary.

> **Losing a job can be the best wake-up call you'll ever get to bring about positive change.**

Just stop for a minute and really think. Maybe it's the right time to be courageous! If your life has taken an unforeseen turn at fifty, or at sixty, consider that your best years may lie ahead if you're willing to shake up the status quo. Even raising school-age children need not be a deterrent to exploring your future life choices.

My grown children remember hearing in their youth that we were moving from sunny Florida to where? Indianapolis.

"But why, Mom? We don't know anyone there!" I convinced them that within one month they would know their new classmates. They would have new friends. I was right, of course.

Seven years later we had the same conversation when we were moving to Wellesley in the Boston area. You know what? Children adapt much more easily than adults. If they have been raised with love and emotional stability, they can adjust to a new situation and even consider it a new adventure.

My son Steven has told me that going through his teenage years in the Midwest changed his outlook on people and life forever. His maturity brought him confidence in the ability to understand and relate to people from backgrounds other than his own, and helped him achieve great success in his career.

As a family, we moved from Florida to Indiana to Massachusetts and then to New York City. By the time that Cap Cities decided to fire me, my children were either in college or had recently graduated. With each new home, they had become more independent and self-reliant. As young adults they chose specific professions and careers, and have grown to become great parents.

Had I not been willing to commit to a career of upward mobility with a "move on to move up" mentality, I'm not sure I would have developed the deep confidence and inner strength necessary to shake up my own life and charge ahead, at the age of fifty, into the choppy waters of small business ownership.

Part Three

THE ENTREPRENEUR

I Was Green Before Green Became Cool

Everybody needs a friend who believes in them; I am fortunate to have this friend. I first met Bren Simon when I lived in Indiana, and our friendship has continued to this day. She is probably the most generous person I have been privileged to know. Back when I was fired in New York, Bren knew the truth about me: she knew of my crumbling marriage, my unemployment, and my mounting fears.

One day she knocked on the door of my New York apartment. When I opened it, she came in and said, "Phyllis, it's over for you here in New York City. You're in your fifties. Forget about finding a new job. These companies can hire two twenty-five-year olds for what you would expect to be paid. Here's the key to a condo in Ft. Lauderdale, Florida. We own it but don't use it. Go to Florida, live in the condo, and start your own business." The clincher was when she said, "And I don't want a penny for rent as long as you live there."

Four weeks later I bought a one-way ticket to South Florida and the early days of Green Advertising became a reality.

The nearby Ft. Lauderdale Art Institute was a great

source for talent, and our first logo was created for $200.00. With an almost bare bank account and structured as a sub-chapter S Corporation, we were in business! I bought an IBM typewriter from Home Shopping Network, found a local Kinko's to copy my proposals, and started to cold-call prospective clients. Local classified ads brought some inexperienced but smart young people to sign on with this new "agency." By paying recent college graduates a low base and a high commission for any clients they signed up, I began to build a small business. Looking back, I didn't acknowledge any doubt or fear; I simply knew that I had to succeed.

Timing is everything in life. This time my timing would be perfect.

Take the Crumbs and the Entire Cake Will Follow

A LWAYS REMEMBER THE TWO KEY terms in getting a new business off the ground: accounts receivable and billing. You can make contacts, write orders, and spend seventy hours a week doing the work. If you don't manage the billing and receivables correctly, you will close your doors quickly.

Having worked for corporations for more than twenty years, I gave little thought to cash flow and how it keeps the operational wheels going. I did have the business sense to keep expenses to a minimum, operating out of my loaned apartment for almost six months.

The copy machine rested on the dryer; the IBM Selectric typewriter, ordered from Home Shopping Network, sat on a portable rolling table. Three additional telephone lines constituted my overhead. Next was my sales force, although that makes it sound much too professional.

I hired three young people at a salary of $100 weekly, but with a guaranteed commission of 30 percent on the net profit of all the business they were able to generate. The 30 percent was easy to guarantee since there was so little overhead; plus I needed to motivate these young people. With a new logo and lots of guts, I had Kinko's print a batch of business cards and stationery. I "trained" my sales force in media sales by asking a few local TV and radio stations to have their reps meet with the newest agency in town and pitch their stations' programming and ratings. In addition to learning about this new media market, the meetings and presentations instilled knowledge and confidence in these youngsters. Although we were in the infancy stage, we appeared to be a grown-up agency.

To enhance our credibility, I kept my New York City answering service. Only now they would answer "Green Advertising." I reasoned that having a 212 area code on my business card would indicate that this new Florida agency had roots "up north." Remember that it's the perception of previous successes that go a long way when you're starting a business in a strange city. It's interesting how the next few months evolved: there was that case of the strip club …

Young Matt called upon a local "gentlemen's club" otherwise referred to as a strip club. Their evening business was solid, but they wanted to promote their buffet lunches as a new revenue stream. The ladies, the runway, and the entertainment were the same, but it was difficult to draw a male lunchtime crowd to the location.

I joined Matt on his second call and sold the owner on the concept of running a TV campaign during sports shows to reach the male viewing audience. I then convinced a TV station to videotape on-site footage of the entertainment, but to keep it tasteful. That was not an easy task.

The club was seedy but the lunch buffet was good. Still, it was all about showcasing the entertainment...that is, the female talent. I quickly learned where the girls kept all those dollar bills handed to them, and how much "the house" took each day. But of much greater importance, the business produced a steady cash flow. I would climb three flights of back stairs to collect my service bill every Monday morning without fail, and was happy to learn that their lunch buffet business was growing each week.

I never imagined that a "gentlemen's club" would be our first client, and as it turned out, our only client, who paid their bills every week without fail, giving new meaning to the term "cash flow"!

To Bed, or Not to Bed

RETAILERS ARE ALWAYS A STRONG source of ad revenue, particularly in the type of growth market of South Florida at the time. One of the largest retailers in this region was a chain of bedding stores which consistently advertised with full-page ads. The chain's owners needed to advertise week-in and week-out to maintain their sales momentum against a competitive climate.

The name of the chain was Sleep-o-Rama and the owners were Mark and Steve Solomon. Despite weeks of phone calls and many letters, they would not find the time to meet with me. Finally, I convinced the owners that I had a brilliant new marketing concept and to grant me just a thirty-minute meeting. The day came and Steve said, "Well, Ms. Hotshot Ad Person, what can you tell us that's so new and different?" I explained that the chain needed to separate itself from the competition and have a strong identity. I had consulted with a talented copywriter and recording personality who thought of a character that would command a radio presence.

Bob Labeskus, a local talent, created the genius concept of Rama, the God of Sleep: Rama who guided intelligent god-like decisions on where to buy your bedding; Rama whose voice the audience would hear on radio spots; Rama who would help raise co-op money from mattress manufacturers to promote a heavenly sleep experience!

I found a freelance art director in the Yellow Pages (no Internet then) and hired him to draw Rama and create spec newspaper ads. Fortunately, about two weeks before, I had rented an office of three small rooms in Pompano Beach, Florida, about six miles from Sleep-o-Rama's offices. It was time to move on from the condo setting and the office space would provide some credibility. My new client insisted that before he would sign an agreement, he wanted to actually drive behind me and follow my car to our advertising offices. He explained that here, in South Florida, many people were not who they seemed, and he wanted to be sure of our legitimacy before he signed the dotted line and wrote my first retainer check.

As I drove back to the new office, with my first client in the rear-view mirror, I called my freelance art director and quickly reminded him about the travel agency just across the hall from our small office. There were three full-time employees in the travel agency and he asked them to please come to our office for thirty minutes, to sit at the table and two desks we had placed in our new office and "look busy."

That afternoon we looked like a real advertising agency. After three meetings and lowball pricing, we had our first retail client.

That afternoon we looked like a real advertising agency. After three meetings and low-ball pricing, we had our first retail client, and Rama, the God of Sleep, became our first success story!

Fear is the best motivator when trying to build a new business. I printed a poster for my office with five simple "Rules" that served as a daily reminder of the path I had chosen. Today we have an overload of advice for unemployed professionals. Join LinkedIn. Polish your resume. Invest in a new wardrobe. Join various networking clubs.

It's true that becoming an entrepreneur is not for everyone. It takes courage and a belief in you. Most of all, it takes overcoming the fear of failure. People in their fifties have forged their careers for thirty years. And the key intangible reward that many fail to recognize is the knowledge and the talent you now possess. The years spent delivering profits for others, can now be invested in yourself and your future.

The Five Rules to Grow a New Business

1. Be courageous. Strike out for yourself.

2. Stay with what you already know.

3. Do what you do best.

4. Don't take any partners.

5. Believe that you will struggle, survive and prosper.

Follow the Money and You'll Find New Business

"Passion is energy. Feel the power that comes from focusing on what excites you."

Oprah Winfrey

THE FIRST FEW MONTHS WERE tough, but I learned that it often takes twenty *no*s before you'll hear a single *yes*. I was not afraid of cold calling and having doors closed in my face. But whom to call?

Slowly realizing that, in addition to department stores, the biggest print advertisers in Florida were real estate developers, I drove around new communities every weekend, from dawn to sunset. Florida residential real estate was booming in the late eighties and nineties. Developers continually advertised with full-page ads in newspapers and magazines to attract potential buyers and lure them from competitive new communities.

But how do you establish credentials in an industry where you have no track record? Easy...you give it away! I attended a number of real estate seminars to learn more about the sales and marketing process in this industry. I became familiar with real estate terminology and buzzwords. I then hired a freelance artist to create "spec" ads for a number of real estate developers, based on what I had seen in their print campaigns, knowing we could be more provocative, timely, and creative.

The goal was to secure three real estate clients in one month. I succeeded in signing contracts with two who were impressed with the fresh approach, but perhaps even more impressed with the low fees we charged.

And as the real estate industry grew more robust, so did the agency.

The world was not waiting for another advertising agency. I knew that I would work very, very hard to stay in business past that first perilous year. I knew that I would stretch out my meager savings in order to build a business with actual, paying clients. I didn't know that when you're the boss, you're mandated to make every decision. After thirty years of corporate life, I always reported to someone above me. No longer. I felt an exhilarating sense of freedom for the first time in my life. And that freedom fueled a passion to set new goals for myself; to tell myself that nothing was impossible; to dare to dream of success.

Over the next few months, gradually building an industry reputation, Green had four developers on a monthly retainer basis, and we were off and running.

You Really Need a
Business Plan—Or Do You?

THE BUSINESS WAS GROWING AND this presented its own set of challenges. I had to hire more talent. I had to figure out how to maximize our growth potential. I had to manage the growth wisely and increase profit margins. I was reading serious business books emphasizing that every new business must develop a business strategy and plan in order to succeed. But not all experts agreed.

While trying to plan my concept of developing an advertising agency in South Florida, I received more advice than I could absorb.

"You need a business plan to serve as a road map if you want to make a success of any new business."

"Don't just open your doors and expect miracles."

"Seek out a banker's advice or look for mentors from the business community."

The problem is that the more advice you hear, the more hesitant you are just to charge forward and go for it!

That is until I spent a memorable weekend at Casa de Campo in the Dominican Republic. Along with George

Hamilton, I was a guest at the beautiful oceanside home of my friends, the Simons. Their home was spectacular and despite the uncertainty of my future, I tried to enjoy myself. After a few days of fun, sun, and golf, I felt brave enough to ask these accomplished people how to develop a business plan for a new boutique-style advertising agency in South Florida. I explained my apprehensions, my concerns, my hesitation, and my inability to craft a solid business plan.

Their reaction was surprising! What business plan? Who needs a road map to get customers? Why talk to other people who have lost their jobs and want to reinvent themselves? Why waste time with a plan when you could be literally knocking on doors and cold-calling potential customers? The conversation startled me, but also seemed to make cold, hard sense. If the name of the game is new business, new clients, new customers…why spend time writing out twenty pages of plans, tactics, concepts, and objectives?

> **If the name of the game is new business, new clients, new customers…why spend time writing out pages of plans and objectives?**

I knew how to cold-call for new clients, but I no longer had the ABC-TV umbrella over my head. I was out there alone, convincing business owners that I could market their products and thereby increase their business to a greater number than they presently were experiencing. I knew retail well, and that retail owners have to be continually nimble to outperform their competition. Unlike mid-size or large corporations where it may take months to reach a decision-maker, retail owners were more accessible. And, if they trusted that you knew their product and their customer base, *and* could do their advertising better and cheaper, you might influence them to "give you a try." That's all I needed to know.

I didn't need a business plan; what I really needed were thirty-six-hour days!

I Needed an Edge

OK. I was convinced that I didn't need a business plan. I *did* need to work really hard, cold-call potential clients, keep my young and underpaid sales force highly motivated, and continue to be optimistic.

I would see print ads in newspapers and magazines and knew we could do better; the same for TV commercials. One day, after seeing commercials for colleges flooding local TV programming, I naively called nearby Broward College and asked for their marketing office. That's when I learned the meaning of the initials RFP and the significance of these initials within the new world I was navigating.

No entity governed by municipal or state laws awards an advertising contract without developing a detailed RFP, or Request for Proposal.

This document states the objectives of a specific project; the capabilities and expertise required of a company to respond; the timeline for awarding the contract; and a specified fee schedule for a respondent to submit. Wow, this seemed to offer a whole new world of potential clients. But how could our little agency get invited to the dance?

I discovered that the state of Florida (as well as other states) assigns favored categories to so-called disadvantaged business. How could we qualify and where were we disadvantaged? Plowing through hundreds of category documents, I found the MBE program. Women were considered a minority at the time, and the Minority Business Enterprise program was developed to help minority businesses gain traction in developing a relationship with a governmental, municipal, educational, or civic entity. If the size of the certified MBE was a deterrent to managing a large governmental account, the MBE was often offered a small minority role with a major non-MBE respondent to equalize the playing field. This "role" was equated to points; thus some RFP documents listed five or ten extra points to an application if they showed an ongoing MBE relationship.

I also learned that the application process was tedious and cumbersome, but what could I lose? Four weeks later, the eighty-page application document was finally sent to Tallahassee with a silent prayer. Within ninety days, Green Advertising proudly became a certified MBE, and that was just the beginning.

The "Sunshine Law" is a Florida law which, among other things, mandates open and transparent presentations to firms submitting a response to an RFP, where applicable. One month after our certification, the Tourism Department of Greater Ft. Lauderdale held open presentations for the many major agencies that had responded to their recent RFP for a three-year contract. The open hearings were at the nearby Convention Center. That day, I dressed in my best business suit and drove to the Convention Center, preparing to be impressed by the "big boys" of the state's leading advertising firms.

The "boys" were out in force. I was overwhelmed and intimidated, but at the end of the day, I had an epiphany: not one agency mentioned an MBE partner in their presentations; this might prove to be our first opportunity. Managing to introduce myself to each president or owner at the reception that followed the final presentation, I privately told each of them of our new MBE status, followed by a quick "elevator speech" of our capabilities.

The contract was awarded to the largest area agency at that time: Harris & Drury Advertising. Four weeks later I answered my office phone to hear, "Phyllis, this is John Drury, president of Harris & Drury. We need to talk."

And so began our journey as an MBE minority partner, participating in marketing a major tourism account. Within two years, we responded, this time by ourselves, to an RFP for Ft. Lauderdale/Hollywood International Airport. The competition was tough, since it involved a solid three-year contract that included nearby Port Everglades, home to twenty major cruise lines. The process was challenging, but I reminded our team that now we had an edge. We were not only a certified MBE—we now had tourism experience.

As is said, the rest is history. We won the airport and port accounts with our great creativity, innovative media planning, and meticulous timelines. And yes, the extra points put us over the top!

As for Broward College, they are now one of Green's top accounts. We're on the first year of a solid three-year contract.

Who Has Time for Cancer?

T ALK ABOUT CURVEBALLS.

I had the motivation. We were gradually acquiring new clients through recommendations. We were paying our bills. Our reputation was growing. The future looked brighter than ever on the day that I learned that my biopsy proved to be malignant.

There is never a good time to hear that you have cancer. And the timing was truly appalling. Like most women, I was at first more concerned with losing my hair than surviving this dreaded diagnosis. Then I learned about the treatment protocol and became even more determined to handle the situation by minimizing its impact on the company: no client would know of my condition and we wouldn't miss a beat in business. The treatment protocol in the late 1980s was simple: The chemotherapy was administered twenty-four hours a day. That meant being hooked up to a machine for two weeks. Solid. Today, of course, there is outpatient therapy that is much more tolerable for the patient and easier to manage.

Combined with daily radiation treatments as well, it was

a rough and tough time for me. I carried on "business as usual" as best I could. Remember, no laptops in those days, so I rented a fax machine to bring to my hospital room. On Fridays, my office manager would bring the company checkbook and a folder of accounts payable, which we'd review after my morning radiation treatment. After I signed the checks, she would leave me to my wires, my tubes, and of course, the constant blare of the television.

We were then a company of four people, and they were the only four people in the world, other than my physicians, who knew I had cancer.

When you head a small company and your employees learn of a potentially life-threatening situation, how do you keep them motivated and on course? My strategy was to appoint a new president of our company and change my title to Chairman. Restructuring the team was easy; delegating authority was not. I convinced our group that the new president would lead them to greater heights and more business opportunities. He was younger than I by fifteen years and, with his newer tech skills and given the rapid evolution towards computerized software, he was perfect for the promotion, and the raise.

I purposefully "forgot" to tell my faraway children about my condition, and soon realized that the attitude and behavior of pure denial was actually making me stronger through the ordeal. When the "wig and turban lady" came to my room, I told her, "Sorry, I'm not interested."

So with great oncology care and a measure of good luck,

I was able to leave the hospital in a few weeks. This was followed by more weeks in treatment until I was finally finished. The follow-up testing went well and I learned that the sweetest words in the English language are "negative" and "normal."

We were then a company of four people, and they were the only four people in the world, other than my physicians, who knew that I had cancer. I gained strength and even more resolve that our growing business would not only survive, but prosper. Just as I had.

P.S. I didn't lose my hair!

Ask for the Business, Even on Top of Aspen Mountain

THERE I WAS, IN THE early years of my business start-up, in a room full of extremely wealthy and successful people. Even more intimidating was the setting: a lavish home at the top of Aspen Mountain. The party was hosted by Les Wexner, of The Limited and Victoria's Secret fame. He had become one of the most successful retailers in corporate America. Many Hollywood luminaries, such as Sean Connery and the billionaire producer Marvin Davis, were there, as well as Wall Street executives and just plain ordinary millionaires.

Despite the powerful corporations and political entities that these guests represented, I thought there must be an opportunity to connect with at least one guest who could lead to future business for my new company. Then I found him: Murray Goodman, the owner of the chic and upscale shopping complex called The Esplanade located on tony Worth Avenue in Palm Beach. The center, anchored by Saks Fifth Avenue, represented many of the most fashionable retailers on the Island, a collection of expensive boutiques and intimate restaurants.

It took two large glasses of red wine, but I finally summoned the courage to ask if I could meet with him the following week, at his office in Palm Beach. Hastily explaining that our new Florida marketing firm represented a unique style of retail advertising, I told him that all I wanted was fifteen minutes of his valuable time. He seemed surprised and confused but ultimately said yes, and that first meeting started Green Advertising down a new and exciting road of retail sales.

I learned that, given the opportunity, you should never be afraid to ask for the business, no matter the surroundings. You might not always get the response you want, but as they say in new business seminars, "Your first *no* is just the beginning of a new sale." This time, although I had feeble expectations, I asked for the business and received a *yes*.

Gaining a foothold in the retail sector was the key to attracting future business to the agency. Many new businesses and firms fail to diversify their client base, and can fall victim to a downturn in one specific sector of the economy. In hindsight, we didn't pursue the retail sector as aggressively as we should have. In later years I Iearned this difficult lesson when we almost closed our doors as Florida's real estate market turned soft overnight.

Watch Your Back by Watching Your Books

IT'S CALLED "RECEIVABLES" FOR A reason. You're supposed to receive money for the services you provide. In the early days of Green Advertising, we would simply be thrilled to *have* a new client. We would be honored that they trusted us with a project. We would be ecstatic when they liked our work.

This mindset and attitude turned out to be a huge mistake.

The billing for client services was entrusted to Mary Ann, our office clerk. She had a myriad of mundane responsibilities and creating invoices was not one of her favorite tasks. Therefore, it was quite common for her to invoice for our services long after the project was completed and delivered.

What was the problem? While our client base was growing, our bank account was dwindling. We were quickly approaching a danger zone for small start-up businesses: the time lag from client acceptance to billing to receiving payment sometimes approached three to four months.

That's when I learned about the world of "receivables." I became a self-taught expert on spreadsheets and thirty-day, sixty-day and ninety-day receivables. It quickly became clear how fast a business can descend from a healthy and promising future to red ink. And all because the owner did not recognize the importance of billing and receiving as well as the importance of a continual "collection" plan created to remind those delinquent clients of the need for payment. We began to pre-bill for a percentage of our projected fees to ease the time lag and gradually converted most of our clients to a retainer-based relationship.

I hate to admit it, but when I first heard the word "retainer" I thought of a law firm. We considered ourselves to be creative types developing print ads, commercials, and logos. Why would anyone pay us a retainer? I changed my thinking after attending a series of seminars focused on, "Why Businesses Fail." After the first session, I knew that I didn't want to become another statistic and learned a valuable lesson.

It makes common sense to evaluate your services fairly and develop a rate card that is appropriate for your industry. But like so many newcomers to the small business world, I initially failed to acknowledge that "services" included client meetings, copyright research, vendor coordination, lengthy conference calls, and all it takes to create that winning ad or a viable marketing strategy.

We eventually promoted Mary Ann to Manager of Client Services and developed a job description starting with, guess what—"Client Invoicing"!

Jack Welch, former CEO of General Electric Co., said it best when he stated: "You can have all the profits; just give me the positive cash flow."

Growing Big While Thinking Small

A *HARVARD BUSINESS REVIEW* ARTICLE BY John A. Welsh and Jerry F. White states that "a small business is not a little big business." Although our firm was eventually acquired by the world's number one advertising agency holding company, our successful business philosophy was to maintain the entrepreneurial principles that made that acquisition so attractive years later.

Entrepreneurs must get it right the first time. There is no margin for missteps and breakdown will quickly result if the company fails to achieve a consistent return on investment. Thus the entrepreneur must constantly evaluate the effectiveness of all investments, which can run the gamut of the company's needs. These investments may be in self-promotional efforts, the buying of newer equipment, or the hiring of additional art directors and account executives. We learned what every business owner should recognize: that every new expense must achieve a significant and accountable return.

Here are our five guiding principles to the concept of "grow big but think small" and staying focused on the road to profitable growth.

Grow Big but Think Small

1. Many of our sales leads do not come from our sales team of account executives. Every staff person is attuned to new business opportunities. Marketing is a twenty-four-hour mindset.

2. Our clients are constantly made aware of our new fast-changing web services, video services, and digital expertise. We are diligent about separating our capabilities and services from those of our competitors. If we don't continually promote our uniqueness, no one else will.

3. New clients are more attracted to our company for our expertise than for our prices.

4. We don't "rinse and repeat" our prospect database. We continually add prospects and carefully prune and delete those names that are time-wasters and no longer have potential.

5. We define and showcase a consistent image to promote our company. As the web-based, digital world evolved, our company name also evolved, from twenty-five-year-old Green Advertising to GreenAd.com to better showcase our relevance to marketing products and services. GreenAd.com became the parent company of Green Advertising, Stalder/Green Advertising, our Orlando, FL operation, and VidPop Productions, our video production complex.

Pertinent to the "thinking small" paradigm is recognizing the importance of passive income which can result in yet another revenue channel. Passive income is not measured in equity time or hourly rates. Passive income is generated when you package the same product or service and resell it multiple times to many buyers. Knowledge is a commodity that should be sold at fair market price. As an asset, knowledge can be packaged to make it worth buying.

A good example of passive income is found in the travel

tour guide business. Many years ago, my friend Judy Davison, a travel agent, became an expert in arranging and selling African safari trips. Sure the trips were customized to the group's size and budget, but in actuality, 90 percent of her package tours were standard and only 10 percent were customized. Judy didn't generate new income by starting with zero-based planning for each new client. She could count on 90 percent of her revenue being passively generated, with only 10 percent sweat equity. As African safari trips became more popular, so did Judy's services as "the African expert."

In the marketing world, media placement is a key revenue source of passive income with a twist. Julie, our director of media, uses her knowledge and media negotiation skills to sell TV, cable, and radio programming to multiple clients of our agency. GreenAd may place commercials for a hospital client, a real estate client, and a college client in the same TV show, because their demographic profile is similar. They need to reach and motivate the same viewing audience. Julie's hours of intense research often result in generating revenue from not one, but three clients.

The time-versus-money dilemma that all business owners and corporate executives face is not easily solved. With a limited number of hours per day, combined with cost increases each year, it's wise to focus on "thinking small" to maximize and leverage existing resources, as well as creating innovative methods to sell your single product or service to willing, multiple buyers.

The Client Diet

W E WERE NOT SATISFIED WITH our profits. We worked
hard to bring on one client at a time. We were doing
fine, but our competitors were doing better. We desperately
wanted to be a resounding success. We needed a daily plan
to reach this goal.

The words that gave structure to our plan were: **The Client Diet**. We live in a world of weight-loss diets, gluten-free
diets, the Atkins diet, and hundreds more. The word "diet"
gives structure to a disciplined plan.

This was not a diet about the care and feeding of clients,
but five rules that were posted on the walls of every office
and cubicle in our company. Yes, even on the kitchen and
bathroom walls! Simply stated, new business and client re-
tention are the lifeblood of every business: how to acquire
clients, how to keep them happy, how to bill them, how to
ensure they pay in a timely manner. The reality is that more
than a million businesses file for bankruptcy every year.
That was one statistic we wanted no part of!

We learned early in the game that being busy doesn't
translate into being profitable. Revenue increases do not

translate into additional profit if the bottom line increases as well.

Here are the five rules that served us well on the road to steadily increasing our profit picture.

The Client Diet

1. Identify those clients that have the best growth potential, and spend your greatest time, attention, and money on the clients that matter most. It will become a worthwhile investment over the years.

2. Create a working environment where people can be honest. Clients do business with people they trust, so ethics and morality go a long way. As relationships develop, your clients will comprehend and identify with your culture more than you realize. Continually reinforce the same transparency and honesty that you nurture within your organization, to your clients as well.

3. Like, even love, your customers. When you love someone, you can't do enough for them. Over-service is always standard operating procedure. Give the client what they pay for, and then give them 20 percent more.

4. Anticipate! The best account executives and sales people have a sixth sense of anticipation. They can smell when a situation may turn south. They are attuned to a client's unspoken words or body language. Never underestimate this quality in everything from negotiation to daily business procedures.

5. Don't be afraid to charge fairly for your services. Clients respect good business practices. They may love being low-balled, but will quickly lose respect if they're getting too many freebies. On the contrary, customers are proud to be doing business with successful companies; your success justifies their decision to choose your product or services.

Be a Chameleon. It Will Pay Off.

WHY DO RELATIONSHIPS MEAN EVERYTHING to service-type businesses? When there is no product to sell, the intangibles of talent, expertise and time are the only products to sell at a profit. That is precisely why relationships are so vital to the health and profitability of a service business. Relationships are built and nurtured on a bridge of trust, structured on a solid foundation of performance and receptivity to the client's needs.

Shakespeare, one of the greatest writers in history, wrote, "To thine own self be true," but Shakespeare never worked in a sales department! As every successful sales or account service person learns, you need a chameleon-like quality to succeed with a diverse playbook of clients.

Becky, one of our experienced account managers, was a whiz at prioritizing client's needs. She knew how to work within our company with the art directors, video producers, and copywriters. Becky never disappointed a client's expectations and timelines. Her meeting agendas were precise and perfect. Her clients, middle managers in large companies, were executives who appreciated her meticulous planning and diligence. They always knew what to expect and were never disappointed. Grading her with high marks at performance reviews continued for several years.

But there was a problem. This problem escalated when our firm was on the brink of losing two key clients.

Becky was almost robotic in her account management performance. This style was successful with the middle managers, but clearly not working with those of her clients who were business owners and wanted and needed more TLC. These clients were hands-on real estate developers who were investing *their* money and *their* reputations when awarding the marketing contracts to our agency. They needed the accurate timelines and effective strategic platforms, but they also wanted to experience a warmer relationship of concern and care. Struggling for years to build their land empires, these self-made business people wanted marketing partners who could feel their pain, could understand the pitfalls of their industry, and would provide comfort and reassurances to the merit of their daily decisions.

The path of least resistance was to reassign these Type A clients to another account person. We had account people who were more personable and exuded a caring vibe while handling the same executive functions. We could always tell when Pete was managing a meeting behind our closed conference room doors. Laughter would erupt periodically and serious clients would hug and kiss Pete before they headed for the front door. Maybe we should shake up our account assignments to better fit the management style of each person?

Not a bad plan, but was it the answer? I've learned

through the years that the path of least resistance doesn't solve the problem. It's a bandage, not a long-term solution.

We conceived a better plan. Along with Court, our president, and with the blessing of our New York-based CEO, we engaged a speech coach (and therapist) for a series of private sessions with each member of our account team. In my ABC-TV years, I was fortunate to participate in semi-annual coaching and presentation sessions. It was mandatory, and for good reason. You may think you're a skilled presenter or a master at conducting high-level meetings. You're sure your knowledge and performance track record will impress and convince everyone in the room.

Well, wait until the first time you view yourself on videotape! Trust me, it's a wake-up call. The sales managers who prided themselves on being extremely serious pros actually looked angry in their playbacks. The more agenda driven people, without much warmth or personality, gave the appearance of prim school teachers instructing a class. When we expanded these sessions to include our creative art directors and motion graphic designers, it was astounding to see such talented people with such poor communication skills.

When there is no product to sell, the intangibles of talent, expertise, and time are the only products to sell at a profit.

Clearly, we were on the right track to improve client interactions by demonstrating to our seasoned and successful team how they were perceived. The succeeding sessions focused on the need to adapt and evolve to each situation, without the sense of simply acting a role.

Our skilled speech coach explained how an inner core of confidence enables you to adapt chameleon-like qualities that relate to another's mindset. Rather than perceived as false and phony, this skill set showcases how the quality of mindfulness is the key to responding to other's needs. The intangible quality of trust is elusive: It takes work and attention.

In our business, we learned how mindfulness meant adapting a relatable attitude to a client. In personal life, it's the key to successful relationships.

If it means being a chameleon, so be it. You'll be first across the finish line when facing the challenges of relationships in your life.

The Client from Hell

EVERY BUSINESS HAS EXPERIENCED THE client from hell. If you're employed by a large corporate entity, you manage to deal with the situation. If you own the business, it becomes personal.

Clients from hell come in all shapes and sizes. But they share one common trait: the ability to make your life miserable.

How you manage the client from hell always involves a trade-off. They may be abusive to your staff, but pay their bills on time. They may be a dream to work with, but never pay until the fifth copy of the same invoice. Or the ego-driven client is never satisfied until he beats the staff into a frenzy, demanding a fifth rendition of a campaign (which usually resembles the first presentation).

The client from hell is never happy, but his money helps fuel the weekly payroll.

In our early years, we had a client who would demand that I come to his office every Friday to get paid for our work. He would throw a check at me and watch me retrieve it from where it landed (usually on the floor). He owned a real estate development company, an industry in which we were just gaining traction. He was arrogant and successful, but I knew his name could open doors to new business. It became an office joke in subsequent years. New clients would say to me, "If your work can please Ken, you can work for me." The trade-off was worth it.

But be wary when the benefits are exceeded by the aggravation. We've had clients show up unannounced and demand to hold a meeting: no agenda, no crisis, just "being in the neighborhood." We've kept clients who continually berated their people while meeting in our conference room, to our great embarrassment. But we've also fired clients along the way.

You have to protect your workers and colleagues and know when to draw the line. One afternoon, Andrew returned to the office in tears after a tense four-hour presentation. How could a one-hour presentation take four hours? Andrew told me the horror story of how the client continually left the room to visit other offices on the floor, and then returned to the conference room, asking him to start from the top. This happened five times! Then the same client buzzed his secretary to bring him a fresh business shirt. He proceeded to strip off his shirt and tie, zip open his pants and change clothes, in front of our account team!

I listened and decided. We fired this client the next morning.

As with most businesses, we've heard threats and dealt with intimidation, even humiliation. You have to weigh the trade-off and determine its value. If the relationship is useful and you come out ahead, keep the client from hell.

You *Can* Buy Self-Motivation, But Where to Start?

"You have to trust in something—your gut, destiny, life, karma, whatever. This approach has never let me down, and it has made all the difference in my life."

Steve Jobs

TO EVERY PERSON WHO IS starting a new business or trying to build a business, the biggest motivation is fear of failure. The daily thought of failure should be sufficient motivation to stay positive, work hard, and understand that seventy to eighty-hour workweeks are the reality.

I learned early in the game that I needed additional techniques and resources to continue to believe in myself. Called constant reinforcement, every small business owner (and it was a small business back then) needs another voice, at times, to continue the task of rolling that stone uphill towards growth and profits. Today, I'd be taking online motivational courses, attending webinars, and Googling self-help tips. Back in the late eighties, to access motivational speakers you attended their seminars, listened to these accomplished speakers, and built your individual diary of instructional steps.

Brian Tracy, a well-known speaker, made a huge impact on me in the early days. At the end of this chapter, I have listed the five key steps that I wrote in my work diary on the last day of one of his 1989 seminars. His messages always struck the same chord but that chord needed repeating. Recognize where you are today. Decide where you can be in one year. Take that out to five years. List your ultimate goals and objectives and then divide these goals into step-by-step subheads. Sounds easy, doesn't it? The truth is that it was an excruciatingly painful exercise.

It was difficult just to recognize that I was charging into unchartered waters: that I was trying to be an entrepreneur for the first time in my life and that I had to succeed in this venture. The alternative was to go backwards to a job at probably half the compensation to which I was formerly accustomed. But I took a page from the Navy Seals playbook: Learn, Exercise, Repeat. Learn, Exercise, Repeat.

And that is what I did with each seminar that I attended.

I also relied upon an equally important motivational technique: playing a set of tapes in my car's cassette player (no CDs then). I would listen to the instructional tapes at the start of each day, and especially on the way to client meetings, where I always needed an extra dosage of confidence. My first set of eight audio tapes covered a broad range of subjects, from confidence-building techniques to the language of business to pricing our services. One day my car was stolen from the small office parking lot. I didn't miss the car too much, since the insurance company paid for a car rental. But I sorely missed the audio cassettes that the thief acquired with the car!

Notes from May 1988, After My First Brian Tracy Seminar

1. I want to earn $100,000 by 1995. (accomplished way before that date)

2. I want to find a wealthy husband. (totally not necessary)

3. I want to build my new company to eight employees. (far exceeded this goal with fifty-plus staff pros)

4. I want to build a successful company that I can merge with or sell to a bigger company. (This took eleven years, until 1999.)

5. I want to be respected and serve as a mentor to younger people. (By the late1990s I was affiliated with a mentoring program at two local colleges: Palm Beach State College and Florida Atlantic University.)

Learning from the All-Stars

I DEVOURED JACK WELCH'S BOOK, *Straight from the Gut*, and learned the importance of team-building and how to develop leadership skills while building and motivating a loyal team. Welch, then-CEO of General Electric, wrote about the candor and courage that true leaders practice, plus how to inspire risk-taking by setting the proper example.

In a more recent book, he focused a chapter on identifying and recognizing star talent. And he astutely noted how stroking a star's ego can be dangerous. I could have written the chapter about how a smart individual will believe they are indispensable and not bound by any rules or company culture.

At Green Advertising we had a creative director who was both talented and charismatic. However, as the company grew, his ego and sense of self-importance turned him into an arrogant tyrant. For almost a year, I endured and tolerated his behavior because, well, he was talented. One day we were reviewing a new campaign prior to a client presentation, and I told him my thoughts regarding what I perceived as the presentation's weakness and what needed changing.

He told me, in front of six people, "Phyllis, your problem is that you are too old to recognize good work. Why don't you go back to your office and pay some bills."

At that moment I clearly realized that he was holding the company hostage. He was so talented we were afraid to offend him, but his belligerent behavior had escalated to the point that it was out of control.

Before I fired this so-called superstar, I confidentially interviewed and hired his replacement. The hire came from within the company as a well-deserved promotion to our senior art director. Although I had waited six months too long, the positive fallout was that our new creative director was rewarded for his loyalty, perseverance, and talent.

Reading Jack Welch's more recent book, *Winning*, was a wake-up call. We were doing some things very wrong. In order to give some people a sense of progress and importance, we often promoted them with new titles. Our company had become too complex with too many layers of management. As our client roster expanded, we increased our levels of reporting responsibility. We were becoming more profitable, but in some ways, more paralyzed. Our organizational chart was a mess.

One day I was looking for Natalie, an account coordinator. I asked Richard, an account executive, if he knew when Natalie was returning to the office. Richard told me that whomever Natalie reported to would know, and he wasn't sure who that person was.

We then had a small twelve-person account team. We weren't Google or General Motors. If Richard didn't know the person between his position and Natalie's, we had a problem. We had too many layers of hierarchy; our growth had fueled new positions and new titles, but less efficiency and effectiveness.

Welch recommends that organizational charts should be as flat as possible. The charts should demonstrate a clear structure of reporting relationships with the emphasis on direct reports that foster meaningful accountability. We clearly needed to make some changes.

The well-known author of *Drive*, Daniel Pink, wrote about intrinsic motivation in this best-selling book. Simply put, intrinsic motivation is when the reward is actually the activity itself, to the person trying to reach an objective, as opposed to striving for a bonus, a salary raise, or a promotion.

Every company wants its employees to adopt a culture which includes pleasing the client, doing one's best, and learning new skills on a consistent basis. It is unfortunate that in most profit-driven

Our company had become too complex with too many layers of management. Our organizational chart was a mess.

companies, cultivating intrinsic motivation is not part of their playbook.

I learned early in the game that paying attention to each staff member's personal goals and business growth was a meaningful time investment. Everyone needs guidance at times, and long-term achievement often depends on the awareness of how to illuminate the daily path of motivation.

We took baby steps to help self-motivate our people. The

measures were simple: hiring a speech coach to improve the presentation skills of our genius creative directors; sending talented account executives to sales training seminars to improve their selling techniques; and sharing monthly financial profit-and-loss statements that had formerly been considered confidential. This last step proved to be the best. When employees have a sense of their impact on the company's bottom line, they will improve their focus to achieve more profit, because the upward tick means raises and year-end bonuses.

Slow and Steady Wins the Race

THE PREVIOUS CHAPTER SHOWCASED THE meaningful attributes of loyalty, perseverance, and talent exhibited by our newly appointed creative director. Working together for twenty-two years, I've been privileged to watch the growth and maturation of this individual—one of the most talented and driven people I have ever met. Let's explore Court McQuire's career track, which may serve as an alternative and instructional guide for today's millennials who look ahead to planning a successful career track.

We read books and articles that define career paths as consisting of between five to eight different jobs in the average career. Yet little is written about having six different jobs within the same company.

With a fresh, new degree from the University of Kansas, Court walked into our small offices asking for a job. Although he was inexperienced, credentials from his college art classes were impressive. Court was hired as an advertising coordinator and soon advanced to assistant art director.

His creative work was good, and his timing was even

better. As our client base grew, our firm's art department expanded.

We always looked within the company first in determining who best could fuel our growth needs. Art directors frequently accompany the creative director to assist in client presentations. In addition to talent and work ethic, good communication skills played a key role in promoting Court to a full-time art director. He was enthusiastic about the advertising business, client demands, and satisfying the challenges of our increasingly erratic creative director.

Advertising has changed more in the last five years than in the previous fifty.

As an integral team player, he worked long hours and weekends to meet deadlines. Meanwhile, our prima donna creative director was spinning in orbit, it often seemed, in a different universe. Court's talent and dedication soon became evident, and it led to his assumption of the mantle of creative director, followed by his appointment as senior creative director. His professional skills soon became obvious as he continued to keep pace with technology.

Court recognized the importance of social media platforms early in the game. To help bring an important client on board, Court impressed them in his presentation by stating, "Advertising has changed more in the last five years than the previous fifty. We are a lean, mean marketing team of professionals. Our motto is: Keep up with technology or GET LOST!" Wow, talk about impact!

He performed true to his beliefs, building a team that

responded to changing technologies and updated software protocols. Always with an eye on the client's return on investment, or ROI, Court was a pioneer in developing branding budgets that balanced the traditional media of unique URLs and 800 numbers with the tidal wave of social media initiatives, interactive, digital, and behavioral sciences.

As Court's star was rising, so was the visibility and achievement of one of our senior account managers. Every ad agency in the world is comprised of two distinct entities responsible for the growth and health of client business: the art department and the account management department. Falling in the middle are specific departments for media, web design, video production, administration, and more.

WPP, as a public company, is rightfully obsessed with succession plans. Our parent company recognized and rewarded growth and profitability, but continually stressed the need and reassurance of a seamless transition from older senior management to younger management at the appropriate time.

Our senior account manager was responsible for adding several large clients to our company roster. His numerous regional and national contacts resulted in an onslaught of several high-profile accounts to the agency. His strengths were highly visible, but so were his weaknesses. He tended to over-delegate to others and avoided difficult conversations and confrontations if possible.

In developing a logical succession plan, it was challenging to determine which executive was best suited to eventually be named president of the company. The establishment of a new president would enable me to assume the much-needed CEO role of Green Advertising, Stalder/Green in Orlando, and Vidpop, our video production facility.

With the advice and blessing of our New York CEO, we promoted both Court and the account manager to new titles, making them equal managing partners. The plan was to determine, at the end of one year, who showed the business skills and team leadership that would take our agency to the next level.

The following year proved more insightful than originally imagined. Court's leadership enabled GreenAd to react swiftly and with precision to the increasingly complicated multi-channel and vertically integrated platforms vital to our clients' brand development and management. He poured over every spreadsheet, scrutinizing line-by-line items, equipment expenses, and overhead costs. He frequently offered meaningful recommendations to replace reoccurring costs and eliminate excessive budgeting in unnecessary areas. I was surprised that cost control became one of his strong suits.

Meanwhile our hotshot account manager, now a managing partner, showed little interest in the "bean counting" side of the business. He managed his accounts with as little effort as possible, relying on assistants and coordinators wherever possible. He appeared to be content in counting down the weeks until his name would be preceded by the title "president."

Does slow and steady always win the race? Maybe not. But Court's professionalism, growth, talent, and dedication propelled him over the finish line. At the end of the year, we threw an office party to welcome our new president: Court McQuire.

Changing the Presentation: Recipe for Success

E VERY SHIP HAS A CAPTAIN. Every school has a principal, and every football team has a head coach. In another relatable context, every accomplished chef depends on original recipes that have proven their success over and over again.

In many service businesses such as Greenad.com, success is measured by a roster full of new business clients. And new business is best achieved by winning presentations, showcasing how our services can benefit another's needs and solving their marketing problems.

After a particularly dry spell of unsuccessful efforts to attract new business to our firm, we took a hard look at the measurable ingredients of our presentation content, context, and style. We recognized there was seldom a clear structure and succinct game plan for our team presentations. The potential client often seemed confused as to who was in charge and who could answer questions and make decisions. This led to misunderstandings and made everyone appear less confident and less professional. These awkward situations did not allow participants to showcase their full skill set and expertise. We were less than a well-oiled machine of integrated activities. On the contrary, many participants would attempt to show they were "the smartest person in the room" by interrupting the agency presenter *and* the potential clients, even presenting contradicting views and approaches within the context of the meeting.

Clients make assumptions based on what they know and what they see. If a team of presenters appears as a harmonious unit, the client assumes that their assignments will be managed with well-orchestrated disciplines guaranteeing efficient and effective results. Preparing for our presentations, we knew our stuff, but often lacked a clear structure and a succinct game plan. We became increasingly aware that a team presentation without a presentation leader was destined for disaster.

Change is difficult. We had talent. We had passion. And we were hungry. Clearly we needed a new winning recipe that would result in fewer losses and more victories.

It was the perfect time to look "outside the box" to examine and expose our core presentation weaknesses. Maybe we needed professional help. You go to a doctor when you're sick, or a dentist with a toothache. We needed an accomplished professional who, being brutally objective, could re-energize our mind-set and bring structure to our style.

Engaging Renate Urban, an accomplished language, communication skills, and intercultural coach, was the first step in this critical mission. Renate's company, Urban Training and Services, works with private individuals and large and small companies to provide communication and intercultural services. As mentioned earlier, her one-on-one sessions with our staff were extremely meaningful in identifying problems with individual presentations and internal interactive communication. Now it was time to pull together and work towards developing into a harmonious unit.

Renate understood our situation and determined that the first step was developing an improved sense of solidarity. She started with the 4S formula for a winning presentation.

The 4S Formula for a Winning Presentation

- Structure: It's under control with preparation that follows a logical structure with smooth transitions, signposts, and mile markers.

- Succinct: Stay relevant and establish a thread of coherent structure. Stick to your line of reasoning. Perhaps use humor to keep listeners' attention.

- Supreme Content: Keep material goal-oriented with a central message around the core purpose, customized to the audience. Visualize the content. Fulfill expectations.

- Stimulating: Keep the listeners' attention at all times with tone, humor, language, and body language. Appear effortless and engaging and entertaining. Be a pleasure to watch!

We understood that with a confident leader who would establish a positive environment, each participant could voice their opinions and deliver their expertise within a comfortable platform. But who can refrain from interrupting a lengthy presentation when they're part of a team? We had opinions and ideas, and in a room full of extroverts, it's hard to remain quiet.

Renate explained how planned interruptions can be positive. Foremost, they give the presenter a chance to breathe and recharge. Secondly, they demonstrate the knowledge and involvement of the team members. The key formula for interruptions is the word "planned." This "give and take" contributes to a lively yet seamless scenario. When planned ahead, it is not disruptive and can help steer the presentation into the right direction with a winning conclusion.

The final initiative involved recognizing our self-image as opposed to other's perception of us. Did the impression that others have of us match our self-image, or should we make adjustments to become better communicators? Communication is a two-way road and we needed to balance speaking and listening. Many of us were trained to give speaking and listening equal amounts of time. We needed retraining to be selective about what we said, and what we listened for.

Improving active listening is really hard. Through my sales training experiences I had learned to observe body language and interpret unspoken messages. (We call it "reading between the lines.") When facial expressions, voice tone, and body language are clearly in sync, the conversation becomes clear and unambiguous. But if these elements point in different directions, words are misinterpreted and listeners are confused.

After much role-playing and team sessions, we eventually absorbed and practiced most of these instructive exercises. Along the way, we became aware that stage fright, or fear of public speaking, is not unusual. The trick is to interpret these feelings as excitement and anticipation. Confidence comes from being knowledgeable and prepared.

When you visit our offices today you'll see signs with just six words:

Be Alert. Be Attentive. Be Sensitive.

One U.S. Senator and
Two Football Coaches

"I'LL WORK FOR FOOD" WORKED for Green Advertising. Small business owners need to be exceptionally creative to quickly build awareness and raise the profile of their business expertise and capabilities.

With a small sliver of profitable clients, we needed a breakthrough concept to generate positive press and shine a favorable spotlight on this upstart agency.

Driving to our new, small office one morning, I saw an unfortunate homeless man at a highway exit holding a sign, "I'll Work for Food." Generous motorists would pause to donate to this lone figure standing in the bright glare of the Florida sun.

The picture of this man haunted me for weeks. How could we spread the message that people were hungry and desperate? How could we help raise funds for our area's food banks and other charities that lent helping hands to the unemployed? The "aha moment" came to me weeks later, and led to the creation and development of one of the most memorable public service TV campaigns in South Florida.

Imagine seeing celebrated sports figures and national politicians holding "I'll Work for Food" signs in a TV commercial to showcase the plight of the unemployed and the hungry in our region? Can you think of huge newspaper ads featuring famous people holding these signs? Well, it really happened!

I first reached out to enlist Florida's U.S. Senator, the esteemed Robert Graham, to participate in this fledging concept. He not only agreed to be part of this print and TV campaign, but suggested that I use his name to convince some of the area's top sports coaches to join him. National Football League coach Don Shula was the next target, and he graciously accepted our invitation. And finally, the University of Miami's head football coach in the early nineties, Don Erickson, agreed to the concept. This completed the "I'll Work for Food" talented trio.

I was confident that convincing the local affiliates of the three major networks to donate TV time would not be a problem. I knew that each FCC-approved station must run a percentage of PSAs (public service announcements) to comply with federal guidelines. My friends at the local ABC-TV affiliate in Miami also donated their production and editing facilities to produce the TV spots. Next was convincing a local photographer to donate his talents and several studio hours to photograph these three renowned public figures. Peter

Small business owners need to be exceptionally creative to build awareness and capabilities.

Langone, a respected Ft. Lauderdale photographer, came aboard and helped create a memorable and impactful newspaper and magazine campaign.

GreenAd was the recipient of many public service awards and press coverage throughout the year. Best of all, donations to the tri-county Food Banks increased by 800 percent for three consecutive years!

The strategic lessons learned here apply to every business, no matter the size.

Lessons Learned

- Dream of creative pro bono opportunities that will benefit the community and will raise the profile of your business. Then find a way to make it happen.

- Don't be afraid to approach the famous. It's easy to get the goldfish, but go for the dolphin. (That's an inside joke, since Coach Don Shula was coach of the NFL's Miami Dolphin football team at the time.)

- Be prepared to reciprocate when you ask for a favor. We told Mr. Langone that he would be our number one choice for ad photography whenever we had a paying client opportunity. We kept our word.

- Select a charity that communicates a clear and timely message.

- Be passionate about the cause. Then you will gladly donate the hours and the weeks to bring your vision to a successful ending.

How Denzel Washington Inspired Me

PEOPLE PAY ATTENTION WHEN AN acclaimed movie star champions a meaningful cause. For many years, this world-renowned celebrity appeared in TV commercials as a powerful spokesperson for the Boys and Girls Clubs of America. His message focused on the many after-school and summer programs provided to children across the country—kids who could not otherwise enhance their abilities and discover new talents and interests. The young Denzel had been given the opportunity to take advantage of the courses at his local Boys and Girls Club. As a famous adult, he continually appealed to viewers across the country to donate and participate in the ongoing funding of these meaningful and worthwhile programs.

Long an admirer of Mr. Washington, I made annual contributions to our local Boys and Girls Clubs, but thought long and hard, for many years, about how our company could make a real difference in the community.

Knowing that the right public service campaign could dramatically raise our company's profile, my thoughts weren't totally altruistic. I continually discussed with Court

McQuire, our company president, how we should create an original public service message that would benefit a charitable organization, and, at the same time shine a favorable spotlight on our company.

One late October evening, inspiration met opportunity.

Daylight Savings Time was slated to end that evening, thereby setting clocks back one hour before midnight. As an avid South Florida golfer, I was bemoaning the fact that the luxury of a 5:00 p.m. round of nine holes would disappear until spring. Now darkness would descend by 6:30 and grow increasing earlier in the coming winter months.

As I started my car, I glanced at the three sets of golf clubs stored against the wall in the garage; my new clubs along with two old golf bags holding full sets of clubs that were in decent condition but had seen better days.

Thinking about how fortunate I had been to receive golf lessons at ten years old, I suddenly recalled Mr. Washington's message about the importance of after-school programs and sports-related activities for the thousands of boys and girls that are provided by the Boys and Girls Clubs across the country.

Wouldn't learning the game of golf be a great learning experience for youngsters in these Club programs? Not just learning to swing a club, but absorbing the etiquette and sportsmanship ethic of the game? Did such a program exist and how was it being handled?

The following Monday morning I called Kae Johnson, the Director of the Boys and Girls Clubs of the Palm Beaches and I told her of my concept: CLUBS FOR KIDS, a program whereby unused golf clubs would be collected to be rehabbed and re-sized and then used by the Club to teach their boys and girls all they should know about the game of golf.

Amazingly, they did have a golf instructional program in place, but sorely lacked golf equipment. I knew how we could reach the many Florida golfers, who, much like me, had unused clubs in their garages, their lockers, their car trunks. This was that rare, perfect fit! CLUBS FOR KIDS be-

came that unique, out-of-the-gate success story I had been hoping for.

The CLUBS FOR KIDS drive was created and implemented by the entire staff at Green Advertising. We convinced two local Simon Shopping Centers to serve as drop-off locations for donations of used golf clubs, with our headquarters office serving as the third location.

Then the fun began: TV network affiliates in our region agreed to run PSAs to promote CLUBS FOR KIDS. Very nice, but we had no TV spots to air.

That is, until we convinced Kae and her team to bring some of their young members to our TV studio to appear as actors in the public service announcement. We wrote scripts and had golf props on hand. The kids were great. They were natural, eager, and professional!

Next, local newspapers agreed to donate large print

space to our cause. This meant that our creative folks used their after-hours time and creativity to develop heartfelt, meaningful print campaigns to inspire golf club donations.

But it still takes feet on the ground to expand every good marketing campaign and CLUBS FOR KIDS was no exception. We knew it was time for some guerilla marketing efforts. During four consecutive weekends our entire staff was deployed to deliver a veritable arsenal of promotional materials and posters to area golf shops, municipal golf courses, and golf pro shops at the many tri-county private country clubs.

Listings on the websites of many media outlets increased the visibility and viability of our inspirational campaign. The message was powerful and consistent. The result? An astounding 6,000+ golf clubs were donated in just sixty days from the time the multimedia campaign took off!

Knowing that the right public service campaign could dramatically raise our company's profile, my thoughts weren't totally altruistic.

With 2,000+ golf clubs and over 300 golf bags in our office alone, the company's efforts generated positive widespread editorial and photography coverage for the efforts of Green Advertising. CLUBS FOR KIDS was never about giving "golf tips." But much can be learned from the experience. There are many valuable no-cost promotional tips for every company seeking to enhance its credibility, raise awareness, and make a meaningful contribution to their community.

Five No Cost Promotional Tips
for Your Company

1. Needs exist for every charitable group and foundation, in addition to monetary donations. Think about "needs" and how your firm can fill those needs with the drive and talent of your staff.

2. Writing a check is easy. Donating brains and time is more difficult.

3. You can spend thousands of dollars in public relations efforts and be disappointed with the press results. Most PR releases get one day's attention. Meaningful, results-oriented charitable campaigns do good works, and live on and on.

4. Robust social media was in its infancy with our first CLUBS FOR KIDS drive. The buzz that social media creates will play a significant role in next year's efforts and we'll be sure to plan for many more drop-off locations.

5. Businesses often tell their people to "think outside the box." This applies to everyone in our society, not just the business world. Accomplishments are unlimited when you let inspiration meet opportunity!

Failure Is Not an Option:
The Struggle to Survive

W ITH THE EXTREMELY ROBUST BUILDING economy of the 1990s, our company flourished. Florida's buoyant residential housing market may have been a bubble, but it was a very large bubble that lasted for a very long time. Our expertise in attracting buyers to country club communities, condominiums, new single-family communities, and hundreds of new townhome developments made us the number one go-to marketing firm for significant developers and builders.

We won hundreds of national awards, delivered record profits to our WPP Group corporate offices, and were offered new projects in far-flung areas such as Las Vegas, Houston, Santa Barbara, and Chicago.

But the bubble was destined to burst. And it did. In Las Vegas, hundreds of buyers lined up inside Bellagio's ballrooms for the privilege of offering a down payment check on a never-to-be-built luxury condominium. In Houston, the affluent marketplace was the perfect setting for a dream condominium whose smallest unit provided over 4,000 square feet of living space. Planned to tower thirty-five stories over the city, the vision of these developers eventually turned into a financial nightmare.

In Florida, home to some of the biggest country club communities in the nation, golf course views suddenly became less desirable and mortgage financing became scarcer for even affordably priced townhomes. Builders went bankrupt. Developers fled the state. And some banks never recovered from the mortgage debacle that easy money had created.

For many years banks had offered "ninja loans." Translation: "No income, no job, no problem. We'll find a way to help you buy your dream home." What started as a slow trickle of client loss in the first year of the great housing meltdown became a tsunami of clients closing their doors and not paying their bills. Our company became haunted by client bankruptcies.

The economic downturn in Florida and throughout the country led to a massive wave of firings. Every company felt the need to downsize and we were no different. It seemed as though almost overnight, we slid from forty-two employees down to twelve. It makes sense that firing someone for non-performance would be a more difficult task than firing a good employee for a situation over which they had no control. It is exactly the opposite. Just like many years ago, when I was in a mindset of denial during my last weeks at ABC-TV, I found that each of our good employees thought it would be someone else, not them, who would suddenly be unemployed.

Our sole objective was to keep our doors open, functioning with good talent and good creativity for our shrunken and crucial client base. With a constant eye on that goal, I mastered the ability to tell some very good and talented people that we could no longer afford their salary. I learned to keep a box of Kleenex nearby, because the employee reaction would range from anger, to disbelief, to tears. The difficulty was not only in losing good people and having to deal with their fears, but in maintaining a positive, upbeat internal business climate where those remaining would give their best efforts every day.

The wisest advice I would give to other leaders in this situation is to show as much empathy as you can and to allow triple the time you would normally figure for this type of meeting. People need to talk and talk: some need to talk out their anger or frustration, others need encouragement and guidance, and still others need all of the above. In essence, the longer the meeting, the better the outcome for both you and the employee.

The final word on downsizing when the economy tanks, is simply that most business owners and executive managers wait too long to trim staff and cut expenses. There is always that sense of optimism that new business is just around the corner; that the stock market will quickly rebound; that the economy will experience a speedy turnaround. Business books contain hundreds of sad stories of huge corporations that did not recognize adversity and react in a timely manner. The same holds true for smaller businesses. There is no quick fix for a sinking economic cycle that could take years before an upturn. But you need to find every possible way to keep those doors open! And be prepared to celebrate when you start hiring again!

Keeping the Doors Open

1. Trim overhead until it hurts.

2. Discover and implement creative compensation strategies.

3. Lower your prices, not your product.

4. Get out there and drum up new business.

5. Motivate and continually demonstrate appreciation for your smaller, loyal staff.

The Knock-out Punch

"The difficult we do right now. The impossible takes a little longer."
Unofficial motto of the United States Seabees

EVERY BUSINESS MUST PLAN FOR a crisis: the loss of a
major client to the competition, the defection of a key executive, a bankruptcy filing by a client who's on your books
for a six-figure receivable. These are all difficult scenarios,
but the grounded business leader focuses on damage control, repair, and replacement.

However, no amount of planning could prepare our company for the crisis we faced one October morning. Mindful
that we were in Florida's "hurricane season", we dutifully
developed a disaster plan to which nobody paid much attention after it was crafted and emailed to all. Communication was crucial to the plan: We knew how to locate each
other at any critical time. We lived in a world of cell phones,
texting, IM, and Facebook messenger. How amazing to comprehend that overnight, our secure world could change so
dramatically!

Hit by Florida's most devastating hurricane in more than three decades, our normal communication channels were severely damaged. Hurricane Wilma not only knocked out cell phone towers, but for many days, major roadways in our area became unsafe and impassable. We suffered not the horrible aftermath of Hurricane Andrew, where entire Florida cities were leveled, but severe enough damage to paralyze almost every normal activity in a large geographic area.

I found my way to our office by a circuitous route the next morning, only to discover huge trees and branches covering every foot of the parking lot, as well as our doors. Another brave soul, our creative director Octavio, was standing in the middle of the parking lot looking as dazed as I felt.

Would you believe the near impossible...that ten hours later we were up and running?

A call on my cell phone (that somehow still had power bars) from Suzy, my daughter living in New Jersey, brought instant clarity to our confusion. "Mom, Wilma missed the Orlando area. All's fine at your Orlando office. Call your manager to buy two large gas generators for same-day shipping to Boca Raton. And be sure the driver brings plenty of full gas containers, and some milk, as well as fresh fruit and vegetables." As a lawyer, she's trained to find easy solutions to complex problems. By day's end we had rigged up six computers to run off the generators, making some media deadlines by minutes. And to our working parents, the fresh food was a godsend.

With banks and ATMs closed for almost a week, the New York office of WPP Worldwide found the answer to our staff's cash flow problems. The Orlando office received a wire transfer the next day, and with a sack full of cash, the Orlando manager rendezvoused with our comptroller at a rest stop on Florida's Turnpike. Two hours later, everyone in our company had $500 cash in their pockets. But getting to our office took creativity as well. The local newspaper, *The Sun Sentinel,* featured a story about our staff, and how GreenAd's means of office commute were biking, skateboarding, and hiking for many days!

A novel twist to the plot of our very own "survivors" story was how one of our employees, who lived forty miles north, collected everyone's cell phones at day's end to power up at home, and then returned the now-working phones to office staff first thing in the morning. Without lights and air conditioning, it was never business as usual. Our account and media teams moved chairs and tables outside each day, cutting deals, booking media, and keeping our clients happy and upbeat.

We all learned a lesson: When you empower your colleagues and employees to tackle a real crisis, unity, creativity, and teamwork will prevail. What seems impossible one day becomes a reality the next.

Culture + Productivity = Profits

M OST BUSINESS CULTURES HAVE A direct effect on the bottom line.

We learned this the hard way. For many years, as Green-Ad expanded from a start-up, three-person shop to a fully integrated agency with a staff of fifty, we became accustomed to nine- and ten-hour work days. Major presentations often translated into weekends becoming work days. "Whatever it takes" was the work ethic. New employees quickly bought into this culture. If they didn't, they quickly became ex-employees. All was working well for us.

A year after the acquisition by WPP Worldwide, we were offered the opportunity to move to larger offices to be shared with another WPP company, the legendary J. Walter Thompson. This original Madison Avenue agency was started in 1864 by William James Carlton. Renamed by James Walter Thompson in 1878, the fabled company pioneered the advertising agency model by hiring artists and writers to form its creative department. Growing to over 10,000 employees in ninety countries, the brand was updated, in 2005, to the initials JWT.

It was a proud day when GreenAd moved into adjacent offices to JWT. We were with the big boys now. Our front-door signage reflected the bond between little GreenAd and the symbol of true Madison Avenue success, JWT.

The rosy hue didn't last long. The first Friday in our new offices felt peculiarly quiet. When I walked to the JWT side I was astonished to see empty offices and cubicles, and the manager closing his laptop, ready to leave. "We close at 2 p.m. every Friday," the JWT manager told me when I asked where everyone was. "We figure that by Friday, everyone here is burned out, and my people need a long weekend to recover."

A surprise to hear, but only the first indication of a totally different working culture than the one to which our staff was accustomed. For JWT, closing every Friday for the three summer months was SOP; closing for two weeks from mid-December to New Year's was also SOP—to say nothing of the staff leaving each day at 4:30.

During our town hall meetings each department head explained their vision of growth, and of potential raises and bonuses associated with profit and growth.

"Hey, we're owned by the same corporation. Why are we shutting down close to seven each night?"

"Why are we open the week before the Christmas holiday?"

"And what's with these Friday afternoon shut-downs?"

These questions never reached my level, but our department heads began to sense a shift in our "normal" work ethic. The proximity of the two companies made it difficult to ignore.

We eventually engaged in a series of town hall meetings where everyone had a chance to speak. Each department head explained their vision of growth, and of potential raises and bonuses associated with profits and growth. We opened our year-to-date P & L spreadsheets to examine productivity and explained the positive financial effect on the compensation of everyone in the room.

The term "culture" can be loosely interpreted. By the third town hall meeting, the GreenAd culture was clear. Each employee understood that our culture led to our profitability, and everyone benefitted as we reached our profit goals.

Never Trip Over Your Own Ego

A NEW UPTURN IN THE BUSINESS cycle? Boy, does that feel great! Your business is booming. New clients are calling. And you're hiring again. Business turnarounds feel damn good. Your executives are pumped each day. Your staff is smiling again. New faces filling up those empty offices are gladly welcomed. The months of bleeding "red ink" are now only a blurred memory.

But wait. You could be entering the danger zone.

Through the years, many business owners who have sensed failure lurking around the corner and yet were able to survive the threat, forget too quickly the lessons they learned during those lean days: what they did each day to survive. They forget how they prudently assessed every overhead expense, no matter how small; how they negotiated less monthly rent and more creative compensation packages for their staff. Business 101 teaches that in order to keep your doors open during a severe economic downturn, you must use tools in your **Survival Kit** every day.

Savvy business owners and managers know these tools will serve even better when business finally rebounds. Sure,

it's easier to handle your payables, but if your vendors have become accustomed to a sixty- or ninety-day payment cycle, why change that time frame now? If your key employees learned that perhaps a few hours on a Saturday were needed to complete a project, why change that? If new guerilla marketing techniques helped your monthly cash flow, don't stop now.

After fifteen years of unparalleled success, our firm had nearly been on the brink of extinction. We could not control the bad economy, but we could create new and different strategies to bring in additional business. And that was the time that egos went "out the door." We developed ten key strategies to find the clients that would help pay our bills in our struggle to survive.

The Survival Kit

1. We contacted every Chamber of Commerce within thirty miles and offered to write monthly marketing articles for their member publications with marketing and media tips.

2. We created a bi-monthly series of e-blasts to a purchased database of business owners and CEOs, showcasing our capabilities AND our incentive pricing.

3. We delegated two different staff members each week to attend every Chamber event and Networking event for a specific week, within a twenty-mile radius.

4. We designed flamboyant business cards and distributed them to be displayed at every UPS and FedEx store that would allow this.

5. We asked for the business. We continually asked, or better yet, nagged our present clients for referrals and letter of referrals.

6. We recommended new, cost-effective projects to our present clients. This might surprise some, but it's easy to overlook innovative ways to drive business when you're so busy focusing on the project initiative and getting paid on time.

7. We rented kiosks at industry trade shows to showcase our capabilities and success stories with displays and handouts to attendees.

8. Meetings with local mayors and commissioners in a thirty-mile radius greatly expanded our profile, raised awareness, and resulted in new business.

9. Where we formerly ignored RFPs and ITNs for presentations if we were not 100 percent qualified, we now reached out to other companies and vendors who could complement our credentials.

10. And finally, we rolled the dice. The company created pro bono work for clients who could not afford our services at the time. We did this with one provision: that when their business improved we would be number one on their speed dial.

Our Survival Kit employed all of the following tactics and strategies. Sure, some worked better than others. But they helped us stay focused on the present and build the future.

Every business owner and leader should create a customized Survival Kit with tools and techniques to use from time to time, not just at critical times, but as weapons to grow the business.

Part Four

HOW TO SELL WHEN YOU'RE ON TOP

Not All Partnerships Are Created Equal

L ET ME WRITE A CRUCIAL note here about partnerships.

In the years of building Green Advertising, I could define the winter season in Florida by the number of inquiries I would receive with offers of huge cash infusions in exchange for a partnership arrangement. It seemed that almost every small advertising agency owner in the Northwest and Midwest was looking for a business foothold in the sunny South. With the lure of a corner office to visit while vacationing, the offers kept coming to my door.

The cash investments were enticing, especially in the early years of constant struggles to keep ahead of my payables. I invested a great deal of time meeting potential partners and listening to their offers. I also spoke to business owners who had or had not taken partners in their building years.

I soon realized the burdens that partnerships carried. My freedom to make client and employee decisions would require a consultation with my partner. My instinctive actions would require the permission of others. The business culture I had so carefully cultivated might be compromised.

I decided to go it alone and found that one of the key rules to growing a new business is: Do not take any partners.

Why Sell When You're Hot?

"Take a chance! All life is a chance. The one who goes farthest is generally the one who is willing to do and dare!"

Dale Carnegie

W HEN WE THINK OF BUSINESSES and companies that are bought and sold, we automatically relate to mega-deals like Google buying a new Silicon Valley startup. Or Yahoo paying billions for a social media acquisition.

What every business owner should know is that for every seller there's a buyer out there. Whether you have a one-person consulting business out of your home office, a fifty-person marketing firm, or a law firm with five hundred employees, if you're making a profit, someone else may want to own you.

Our marketing firm went from start-up to consistent and respectable profits by year four. In the early years we were able to cover overhead, but profit margins were scary and slim. As our reputation and referrals grew, it was good to have a reliable profit cushion month in and month out.

By the thirteenth year with more growth ahead, I discovered that *Florida Trend*, a highly respected regional business magazine, created a yearly list of the "100 Fastest Growing Companies in the State of Florida."

"Mandy," I said to our bookkeeper, "we're growing pretty fast. We have three consecutive years of respectable profits. Check out the requirements for making this list and let's go for it!" Within the next month, Mandy had submitted our application to the publication.

Imagine my surprise when three weeks later we were notified on the Wednesday before Thanksgiving that we had made this prestigious list. Green Advertising was officially one of Florida's Fastest Growing Companies! Unfortunately, I was too busy and stressed with deadlines before a holiday weekend to realize that this accolade would be another turning point in my life.

The invitation to attend a recognition awards banquet was scheduled in Orlando early the following year. The two-day seminar preceding the award ceremony was sponsored by the former "Big 8" Accounting Firms, in partnership with the University of Florida's School of Business.

> The most important lesson I learned was to look for a buyer, or buyers, when your business reaches a new profit peak.

Noting that I was often the only female in the seminar rooms, I took notes at every session, being particularly interested in "How to Sell Your Business." I had never thought of selling my successful business. I loved being president, chief executive officer, and the major decision-maker.

But what I learned was that most small business owners make the same mistake of waiting too long before they
decide to sell a profitable business. Unless there are children
involved who will eventually manage the business, the best
time to sell is when you're hot; when you're making consistent profits each month.

Keep in mind:

1. Most entrepreneurs don't think of selling unless they
    suffer health issues.

2. Some owners wait until their age and energy levels
    become a factor.

3. Some wait until their business starts eroding, due to
    an economic downturn or new competition.

The most important lesson I learned that day was to
look for a buyer, or buyers, when your business reaches a
new profit peak; when you've had a few good years, and
see more good years ahead. That's the time when your business is most marketable and can command the best market
value.

Remember that your business can be just you, in that
home office. Trust me: there are buyers out there who seek
small, profitable businesses to fuel their growth with acquisitions.

Oh, I almost forgot. When the speaker at the "How to
Sell Your Business" seminar had asked for questions following the completion of his presentation, he never acknowl-

edged my raised hand. Instead he called upon eleven men, many with repetitive questions. On the way to the elevator, the man who had been sitting at my side during the meeting told me that he noticed I was taking notes for my boss. He complimented me on being a good secretary!

I drove back to South Florida realizing that I had no faith in using one of the bigger accounting firms to help sell my business. I was convinced that my timing was good. But I needed to be taken seriously, and clearly start the search to find a buyer on my own!

The Plan

FROM A START-UP SUB-CHAPTER S corporation with three people, to a present staff of thirty-five people, business was growing each year. By the late nineties, I recognized that many advertising agencies, large and small, were being acquired by mega-holding companies. Omnicom, WPP Group, and InterPublic were buying up large agencies such as J. Walter Thompson, Ogilvy & Mather, Grey Advertising, and more. But they were also buying smaller, niche agencies.

I had a plan. I would find a smaller boutique agency that might be interested in a growing Florida office. Establishing a set of criteria for my search helped me focus on acquisition potentials. None of the mega-giant conglomerates would be interested in an acquisition as small as our firm, Green Advertising. So my sights were set on a successful agency already owned by one of the mega-giants. I would hopefully attract acquisition interest by showcasing our solid growth track and my good business judgment in expense control.

Through the years, I had heard many sellers' remorse stories and knew firsthand of business owners who rued the day they sold their personal stake to an outside buyer. I learned from hands-on research of the pitfalls that followed selling your business to the wrong buyer. The head of my local accounting firm cautioned me to think carefully before I took this drastic step. Pages and pages of well-known business books raised every red flag possible when contemplating a sale of your biggest asset.

So with all of this well-meaning advice, what's a girl to do? Well, I started by listing the five critical steps to avoid disaster and achieve the success for which I was hoping:

1. **Arm yourself with everything you can learn about a potential buyer.** Knowledge is ammunition and you need to be fully loaded.

2. **Establish YOUR terms for the sale.** Not the price. That's to come. The terms define if you want to sign the papers and walk away; if you want to be involved for a specific time limit; if you want to retain the title, the compensation, and the responsibilities. If you choose the latter, is there a mandatory retirement age? Who calls the shots to determine when you are no longer relevant?

3. **Get to know the buyers.** You can meet people ten times and not actually know them. Take the time to talk to others who know them and/or who have conducted business with them. Ask the potential buyer for financials. If you've proceeded this far it's fair that you get to know their business as well as they

get to know yours. As you listen and learn, process all of the information without emotional involvement. Make a business decision, not an emotional one. And finally, trust your gut to determine if these buyers are good and honorable people.

4. **The Money.** Research and learn what the comparable multiples are in your industry and for your size firm. Don't overprice your expectations, but don't sell yourself short either. Think creatively when negotiating the deal. Creative thinking involves performance bonuses, increased compensation schedules, evaluations, and even vacation time. Once the deal is done and you've signed the last page, the negotiations end. You have to live with the terms and the money. Be pretty damn sure that you can do both.

5. **When you have one deal pretty much where you want it, it's time to look for a second buyer.** What? A second buyer after all you've been through? With firsthand knowledge, I can write that nobody gave me this last piece of advice. The acquisition of our firm was fairly seamless, and twelve years later I am still the CEO. Our parent company is respectful of our efforts. I remain motivated to achieve goals and profits to this day. I'm not sure that I could have negotiated better terms or more money. I'll never know because I never tried. But I would recommend that you do seek out that second buyer. Take a deep breath

and look around. You already have your suitor but maybe there's someone else who is better-looking with deeper pockets. Remember that for every seller, there's a buyer. Do your homework and you'll discover the right one.

Finding Mr. Right

I WAS ALWAYS GOOD AT MARKET research. The clinical process of interpreting data is void of emotion. We would continually use extensive market research to defend a creative platform or position for a client's product or service. The more data that's available to support the creativity, the greater chance of acceptance and success.

Applying the same principles to my buyer search took me in several new directions. Rather than hire a merger and acquisition company, I was determined to find Mr. Right by myself. If he turned out to be Mr. Wrong, I would have only myself to blame. Narrowing my search to three major cities, I studied several boutique and mega-agencies in Chicago, New York, and Miami. Because this was years before Google Search and other online tools, I had to be resourceful and innovative. Imagine writing letters (and mailing them) to CEOs and presidents of far-flung agencies. It was another time and another world!

One of the more interesting responses was from the president of a New York agency owned by the mega-worldwide holding company, WPP Group Worldwide. I learned that

> In just a few short years, WPP acquired many storied, legendary advertising agencies: J. Walter Thompson, Ogilvy & Mather, Young & Rubicam, Hill & Knowlton.

Pace Advertising was the first acquisition of Sir Martin Sorrell, CEO of WPP, a UK-based advertising holding company. Sir Martin had been a vital player in the growth of Saatchi & Saatchi, and, according to legend, was widely viewed as the "third Saatchi brother." Being a visionary and a brilliant businessman, the legend continues that Sir Martin realized he would never be a third brother, despite press stories and assurances. So at a fairly young age, he acquired a small U.K. company called Wire and Plastic Products Plc. To this day, few people know the nature of this small, nondescript company.

However, Sir Martin had an ambitious plan. His plan was to acquire profitable advertising agencies around the world and build WPP into an advertising empire.

WPP's first acquisition of Pace Advertising established the North American presence of this new company. What followed was an industry revolution that had Madison Avenue reeling. In just a few short years, WPP acquired many storied, legendary advertising agencies: J. Walter Thompson, Ogilvy & Mather, Young & Rubicam, Hill & Knowlton. With these giants of traditional advertising safely under the WPP banner, Sir Martin then went on to acquire another industry giant, Grey Advertising. Since some of these acquisitions were highly adversarial, the press coverage of WPP's growth remained

at an all-time high. Many unkind words were quoted and re-
peated by esteemed agency principals who had become quite
wealthy, while surrounded by a sense of entitlement.

I was particularly intrigued by Sir Martin's business culture and its impact on Madison Avenue's traditional "white
shoe" advertising agencies. It was a poorly kept secret that
as late as the 1950s, the mainstream advertising agencies
did not embrace diversity. Talented Jewish copywriters and
artists found an invisible barrier to employment. African-
Americans were nowhere to be seen on employee rosters.
As portrayed in the popular cable series *Mad Men*, senior
agency executives were always male and white.

By the 1980s, as I continually interacted with these mega-agencies in my role as an ABC-TV marketing representative, the agency landscape had evolved to include greater
diversity of sex, race, and religion. But culture is a different
animal. It was the mid-1980s, and the executive suite at J.
Walter Thompson still welcomed the three o'clock tea wagon wheeled around their floor by two African-Americans in
starched white uniforms. Special orders for some bourbon
on the side were easily handled. Unfinished business would
conclude at the end of the business day over martinis at one
of the nearby restaurants or bars. Visits to the company's
lavish Canadian hunting lodge were a perk reserved for
their biggest advertisers.

Along came Sir Martin who recognized a fat payroll
when he saw one. His message, upon acquisition, was loud
and clear. He was a bottom-line executive who would ensure that every acquisition became a "lean machine" and
continually grew more profitable.

When Strangers Meet

I WAS IMPRESSED BY LITTLE PACE Advertising, a forty-person shop whose long profitability record attracted Sir Martin's attention. If this brilliant visionary trusted the solid management of Pace, as WPP's first North American acquisition, maybe I should, too. Subsequent research supported my early trust. I responded to Pace management and arranged to meet, but only on my turf.

I didn't want to be the little lady traveling to New York City, hat in hand, asking questions and hoping for truthful answers. Again, the need to control my destiny paid off handsomely. I greeted Pace's principals in our Florida office with prepared nondisclosure forms to be signed by all. I later learned that they were taken aback by this aggressive greeting, but what's a better time to make a good impression? You only have one chance to make that good first impression.

As first meetings go, it was successful. We arranged to go forward with an exchange of more sensitive documents, and then have a second meeting.

The Pace offer to buy Green Advertising came rather

quickly: It was not good. I was terribly disappointed by their offer and not sure where to turn for advice. I was not a financial wizard, but I knew numbers, and instinctively understood that this initial offer fell short of my expectations.

Enter little Irv Katz, a small, unassuming man whose everyday attire was a beige golf cardigan sweater and khaki pants. Irv was a family friend who also happened to be a retired financial whiz. In his retirement, he continued to manage the trust funds of several of his wealthier friends' children. Millions of investment dollars were managed by Irv from a computer in his home office at a nearby Boca Raton country club community.

Irv felt that I needed protection, and agreed to meet with me. As I sat in the study in Irv's unpretentious home, I could tell he was not happy. After pressing his calculator again and again as he reviewed the Pace offer, he turned to me and said, "Phyllis, I'll meet with these people but only on one condition. You are not to say a word. Not a single word. Trust me to deliver the response in person."

And trust him I did, as we entered my same office conference room for another meeting. After the gratuitous exchanges, Irv opened the meeting by saying, "Gentlemen, this is not an offer. This is an insult."

I almost fell off of my chair. I saw my future riches going up in smoke. Not only was the wedding cancelled, but the dream groom would disappear forever. To my eternal surprise, their response was at first defensive, yet not entirely negative.

Naturally, Irv Katz knew that this meeting and these negotiations were only the beginning. If the suitors had al-

ready made three trips to Florida in just eight weeks, they were not on a fishing expedition. They were serious. But it was difficult to gauge if they expected that their low-ball offer would meet such outright objection.

The meeting was hastily concluded with assurances that they would review Mr. Katz's comments and objections. No future date was set to meet.

"Don't worry, Phyllis," said Irv. "You'll hear from them very soon, and this time, they'll present a legitimate buyer's offer based on market multiples. Remember, they didn't know if you needed a lifeline to stay afloat, so they threw you an inner tube. What we want is a real boat with all the bells and whistles."

Irv's astute prediction proved to be correct. Pace executives were impressed by their visit to our Florida offices.

They liked what they saw. They had hoped for a better response to their offer. But we were in play.

The better offer came three weeks later. The buy-out formula was mysteriously complicated to me, but Irv patiently walked me through the numbers. Pace proposed that I fly to their New York offices to review the terms, this time on their turf. When I finally felt comfortable with my decision, I booked the flight to New York City.

I learned that good business people are *really* good. They know how to sweeten a deal so it becomes irresistible. On a steamy summer morning in July, I sat in the CEO's office at Pace Advertising and reviewed the buyout package and terms once again. By noon, I had accepted the offer and we left for a pre-celebration lunch. When we raised our glasses to the new arrangement, I learned they were awarding me a "signing bonus" as a show of good faith. What a nice surprise!

As the taxi drove to LaGuardia airport, I kept reaching into my attaché to peek at my bonus check. Boy, did it look good.

My Ship Came In

WITH HIS INFINITE FINANCIAL WISDOM, Irv helped me negotiate the deal, from the buy-out terms to my future employment status. I learned that the expertise I needed came from a trusted family friend. Not everyone is that fortunate. My advice is to recognize when you're entering unchartered waters. There is always someone smarter than you and more experienced than you. There's a saying that "numbers don't lie." But if you don't have the experience of interpreting numbers and buyer offers, you can quickly experience seller's remorse. Often it's too late.

Once the general offer terms were acceptable, the next stop was to my accounting firm. I needed to clearly understand the tax ramifications for my four-year buyout so that there were no Uncle Sam surprises at year's end. Yes, there was some sticker shock when the first meeting ended, but better to know than to be blindsided at a later time.

And finally, there's the lawyer. Every transaction needs a lawyer. Knowing that Pace had a high-priced New York-based WPP attorney to represent their interests, I carefully weighed my options. I finally elected to use a local, trusted business attorney with whom I could openly communicate. Greg's firm had created my original sub-chapter S corporation. Now, many years later, he would take me to a new level.

I was giving up ownership. I was losing control.

But I was discovering my new destiny.

Part Five

—————

THE NEXT TRANSITION

Another Choice. Another Challenge.

AN INSIGHTFUL PSYCHIATRIST HAS WRITTEN many books about what he calls "choice therapy." Dr. William Glasser, whose books *Reality Therapy* and *Choice Theory* have sold widely, asserts that people choose happiness by recognizing that only they are in control of their lives.

"Other people can neither make us miserable nor make us happy," he writes, as he explains that "choice theory" teaches that we are much more in control of our lives than we realize. Accepting responsibility for our choices greatly diminishes the tendency to blame others or relive past hurts.

I always believed in the principles of Dr. Glasser's writing. From the time I chose to leave Florida and travel to Indiana, to knowing that it was the right choice to sell my company, I realized that I could control my life. Not all my decisions would go well. But I refused to blame others or relive my past problems and hurts.

Instead, I learned my lessons well. The experiences and challenges of leaving my comfort zone, leaving a city, leaving a job to further advance my career were all difficult choices. Weathering the lean and embarrassing years of unemployment made me more determined than ever to choose to find a path that would help me control my destiny.

We all come to a crossroads in life. Many people have the opportunity to "grab the brass ring" as the merry-go-round of life goes 'round. However, I've seen scores of professionals fail to recognize the opportunity to grab that ring and make a choice that may change their lives.

I had made a choice. Now I faced a new challenge. For me, the choice to once again become a corporate employee presented a challenge of attitude, mindset, and behavior. Could I adjust to a strict corporate structure? Could I evolve my entrepreneurial skills to creatively grow the business under a new and different management style?

I quickly recognized that the many years of relocating to new environments and new companies had provided me with a resilience that would now serve me well. I drew upon the years of adjustments to new positions, new bosses, and new rules. It was never easy. This time, I was determined to make the adjustment quickly and easily.

My decision to sell the company had been based upon sound business principles. Working within this framework should be a piece of cake. So now I had to submit expense accounts for reimbursement. Now I had to seek approval for new hires. Now I had to take and pass the corporate anti-bribery and anti-corruption courses. But at the end of the day, I had a profitable buy-out package, a nifty 401K, and a solid employment contract that would self-renew every two years.

I had made the right choice and knew that I had conquered the perceived-as-tough challenges.

It's often easier to continually look in the rear-view mirror and blame others for your current situation. It's harder, but it's your choice, to dig deep within yourself and recognize the strengths and capabilities that have brought you to a crossroads of life. I knew these strengths and capabilities. But I was now faced with new challenges: what about my inexperience in heading a division of a huge public company? Now I reported to a New York-based CEO and CFO who were fifteen-hundred miles from my office. Now many business decisions were guided by compliance to the Sarbanes-Oxley Act or by the firm control of our corporate Human Resource department.

I never had a mentor. I was always the lone wolf carving out new paths that led me to stay focused and change direction when necessary. Now I really needed someone who "had my back." I needed guidance and solid business advice to succeed, and it was to come from a brilliant business executive who would play a significant role in my future. Milton Bagley, Pace's CEO, would relate to my situation. When he sold Pace Advertising to WPP Group in 1986, he willingly transitioned from owner to a corporate employee. Now, thirteen years later and with many successful milestone markers, Milton advised me to continue to run the business like my own. "Make smart decisions based on your experiences. Do what your gut tells you. You got this far by trusting yourself," he

> **Sir Martin had told my new mentor, Milton Bagley, "I love good news. I can handle bad news. But I never want surprises."**

said. Milton wisely added that, years before, Sir Martin had told him, "I love good news. I can handle bad news. But I never want surprises." He told me to remember these words and be guided by these principles.

The years following the acquisition led to many successes and also some turbulence. I knew I could always trust Milton Bagley with the truth.

At last, I had a mentor!

What Does a CEO Do, Anyway?

MAKING THE TRANSITION FROM PRESIDENT to Chief Executive Officer was inevitable. With our corporate ownership's obsession for a seamless succession plan, the new position of CEO was created when I decided to stay on board after my four-year buyout period was completed. I was uncertain of my new role or new responsibilities. A president's role in a company is clearly defined. Direct reports are accountable to the president, as are department heads as well, depending on the size of the firm.

So what does a CEO actually do? I quickly learned that an effective CEO is equal parts neutral listener, a wise Solomon, and a benevolent dictator. Somewhat removed from the hour-by-hour, day-to-day project and client decisions, I saw a clearer vision of opportunities, performance, and competitive strengths. I became consumed with the focus of achieving profitable growth.

Sure, we were busy: our people worked ten-hour days and we were sought after by new clients. Yet our P & L statements for the past two years were anemic by comparison to our level of activity. "I may lose money every day, but I make it up on volume," is every businessperson's sick joke. Our company was not losing money, but we weren't making much either.

During a particularly contentious meeting I suggested firing a few of our clients. They were nice people with respectable businesses, but they refused to accept annual fee increases. As their work demands grew each year, our profits shrunk.

At another meeting I noted that one of our account executives had a problem retaining a client over a deadline miscommunication. We were wrong. The client was right. However I had "graduated" from the business school in which one builds a bridge of trust and respect with a client so that one unfortunate incident doesn't irreparably destroy a relationship. Had this particular account executive demonstrated such a great record of accomplishment that her inability to save the account was merely a blip on her record? Her supervisor told the group that maybe this was symptomatic of her ongoing relationship problems. This last situation just exploded more quickly, before the supervisor had time for "damage control." We took a vote, and decided she was not irreplaceable. Our company was too small to settle for B-players. We needed superstars who were promotable to the next level.

> **To become a truly effective CEO, I quickly realized the importance of anticipation in managing our many ongoing issues.**

From my new global point of view, many other initiatives became apparent. And most negative issues were resolved before they became significant. I didn't achieve agreement on firing our smaller accounts, but the spotlight on their profit margins was more apparent. Rather than have an unfavorable focus on their business acumen, each department head embarked on a personal mission to explain fee increases to their clients and slowly implement them.

Becoming an expert chess player requires anticipation. Good tennis players exhibit the ability to anticipate the ball's path and prepare to react. To become a truly effective CEO, I quickly recognized the importance of anticipation in managing our many ongoing issues. Corporate compliance and annual audits, conducted externally, headed my list. Without stellar compliance grades and the achievement of passing marks on audits, we would know what trouble really means. I delegated, but oversaw, the lesser issues of adherence to HR services and integration of health benefit programs.

I learned never to delegate employee grievance issues. When they start small, the challenge is to keep them small and solvable. If not, they will escalate and become ugly. The worst case scenario is possible litigation. As a division of a public company, you do not want to face an employee in a courtroom.

Years before, at the height of one of Florida's many building booms, our company opened a small satellite sales office on the west coast of the state. With the best of intentions and a seemingly rosy future ahead, we convinced the owner of a local public relations agency to come aboard and head our new office. Kim was well-liked and well-known in the town: a great hire to generate new business in an area poised to explode with new construction and new housing.

One of those classic "real estate bubble-bursts" hit the state within the next four months. After bleeding red ink with rent and payroll checks for another month, we decided to close the office, offering Kim a reasonable severance package. Not too surprisingly, she retained legal counsel, who promptly rejected our offer. It was a reasonable offer, considering her short tenure, but her attorney thought he could do better. After all, he'd be fighting a mega-worldwide advertising holding company in his local rural courtroom. I envisioned little Kim in her prim business suit testifying to a New York corporate lawyer about her unfortunate situation. She'd probably have a tissue to wipe her tears and a therapist to testify about her anxiety. I remembered her conversations of star-gazing on the beach with her therapist, to feel the influences of star constellations as a personal guide.

We did not want to face litigation in Ft. Myers, Florida. I convinced our New York CEO, who in turn helped our corporate New York law firm understand the need to make the severance package a little fatter, and thereby, more acceptable. Money solves many problems. In this case, the legal issues were quickly resolved. The pending lawsuit was withdrawn. The courtroom file was closed.

So what does a CEO do? The threefold answer is: Anticipate trouble, listen to all sides of an issue, and never walk into a courtroom (unless you are the plaintiff)!

You'll Never Be 100 Percent Ready

IN BUSINESS, YOU DON'T GET a chance: you *take* chances. Successful executives and owners are never 100 percent sure their efforts will work, but they've learned if you wait until you're 100 percent ready, you'll never know what really works.

I've seen very capable executives miss a major opportunity because they've insisted on more research, more time, more knowledge. Most opportunities take us out of our comfort zone, so we hesitate. When we know the outcome, we feel more confident. Differently stated, who wants to fail?

"Success is walking from failure to failure with no loss of enthusiasm," is a quote attributed to one of the most astute statesmen of the twentieth century, Winston Churchill. This proves true in the everyday management of a business. The outcome of every decision made by a business owner or corporate executive results in some degree of success or failure. Often it's a decision that will only yield a positive ROI after many months or years of red ink. But as retail visionary Sam Walton said, "Capital isn't scarce; vision is."

A few years ago, our company painfully examined the

competitive landscape and realized that many other firms could replicate our services utilizing the same cost structure, or even cheaper. We needed to create a new, powerful profit center. We desperately needed to provide new and unique services to our existing customer base and attract larger fish to our pond.

We recognized that integrating the online and offline channels of marketing into one team would allow for a more unified approach, yielding faster results and higher SEO results. Our social media services addressed the importance of continual, appropriate content propagation on portholes like Facebook, YouTube, Flickr, Twitter, Instagram, and more. Now, our eyes turned to providing video content to clients, within a cost-efficient and effective structure. Knowing that video content is critical for SEM and brand recognition, we planned to create an in-house team of pros that would react swiftly and with creative precision to today's unique marketing challenges. With the right facilities, we could continually provide new video content to feed the websites and YouTube channels of our clients.

What emerged from our self-evaluation was the desire and vision to move to a larger location and incorporate an on-site green/screen room and edit suite; thereby creating our in-house video complex. Proving the need for this was the easy part. Convincing our corporate owners to approve the investment was more difficult.

We weren't 100 percent certain of financial success, but we knew that building this complex would meet the one key objective of separating ourselves from "the pack" and could be achieved overnight. As usual, our corporate ownership asked for more research and more projections before they would finalize the funding of this expansion. We did provide some optimistic projections and estimated client revenue, but in the end, took the chance and moved to a great new loft-like space, where we opened VidPop Productions, alongside GreenAd.com. Almost overnight, the profile and perception of our firm took quantum leaps. Incremental revenue followed.

Today, VidPop's video complex runs at full speed over ten hours a day, creating and producing a steady stream of video content. Yes, we also shoot TV commercials, but in today's marketing world, content is king!

We were never 100 percent ready to jump into the future. Had we been exceptionally prudent, perhaps we would have waited. But timing is everything. The golden opportunity for increased visibility and greater revenue might have slipped away because you never know what really works and often can't guess how well!

Face-off in the Multigenerational Workplace

THE TRUE AND UNPRECEDENTED PHENOMENON in today's working world is that of four generations working side-by-side. In years past there was a natural sequence of younger workers entering the working world and reporting to older management who maintained the power and the privilege.

With the shift to a technology-based society, the traditional roles defined by age are often blurred or entirely erased. Exacerbating the age/power reversal are the distinct differences in communication styles, attitudes, sociological, and economic circumstances and the experiences that have defined each generation.

We never realized this until it actually happened. At GreenAd we had four generations dependent upon each other for collaboration and success. In our world, time is money. Communication is vital. Understanding each other and communicating effectively are not a luxury. They are a means to survival and growth.

With an awareness of the importance of this paradigm

shift in the working world, let's examine the four generations.

The Four-Generation Office

The Traditional Generation:	Born before the early 1940s
The Baby Boomers:	Born mid-1940s to 1960
The Gen-Xers:	Born 1960 to 1980
The Millennials:	Born 1980 to 2000

The Traditional Generation is defined by the shared core
values of dedication, sacrifice, hard work, patience, and
honor. Many of this generation remember the first functioning computer, the first organ transplant, and the introduc-
tion of color TV. Their leadership style is one of "command
and control." Legendary leaders like Vince Lombardi, War-
ren Buffett, and Jack Welch evolved from a generation where
the reporting system was clear, consistent, and organized.

The Baby Boomer Generation is difficult to paint in
broad brushstrokes. On the one hand, the country's mood of
optimism and economic growth offered them a new world
of opportunities to pursue their personal gratifications. On
the other hand, this generation discovered a whole new
world model, one which paradoxically included the easy
access to mood-altering drugs, the pursuits of spiritualism
and environmentalism, and the complexities that involved
our country's intervention in Vietnam. Governmental authority and issues of patriotism were never again looked

upon in the same light, and neither were traditional values. Recognizable names associated with this generation are as diverse as John F. Kennedy and John Glenn to Mick Jagger and Jimi Hendrix, but also include business leaders like Steve Jobs.

Most of our department heads are the Gen-Xers, exhibiting the key traits of independence and self-reliance. The decades that separate Gen-Xers from my generation are reflected in their ability to get the work done on their terms, with a casual approach to authority. They understand the dynamic of non-existent job security and hone their talents to market needs, being more technologically savvy than their older colleagues.

Court, our firm's president, typifies this generation with his unique ability to persevere and grow in a continually redefined work environment. Joining GreenAd at age twenty-three, fresh out of college, his first title was that of an assistant art director. Evolving his creative abilities while immersing himself in the business side of the business enhanced his value to the company. He rose to senior art director, then to creative strategist. Two decades later, Court was elevated to the position of president, as recognition of his ability to lead the company into the future.

As the only representative of the Traditional Generation, learning to communicate with our Millennials took on a whole different meaning for me. Many Millennials prefer to communicate with IM or text messages. They can text as fast as they talk! Desiring a large degree of autonomy, this generation helped change many of our policies and procedures. Our group meetings are briefer and fewer, with email and text updates replacing the face-to-face "sit-downs" that used to sap valuable time.

Years back, we realized that Xers can do many tasks at the same time, and do them well. The label *multi-tasking* was born. Today, the Millennials connect on many new and different platforms. With continual interaction through mobile devices or online, their world of social communication differs vastly from their older colleagues. Often accused of having poor social skills, this generation actually communicates more intensely and efficiently than preceding generations.

Our social media marketing department started with a few freelancers who wrote weekly blogs from their bedroom offices. Recognizing the need to continually propagate our client's social media platforms with new, timely content, we hired Andres, a twenty-six-year-old social media communications expert who developed a content calendar to expand the profile of our agency and that of our clients.

Each staff member at our firm is mandated to post weekly blogs and maintain active Facebook pages. The myriad of continually new platforms is integrated into Andres' daily schedule and reflected in the increasing demands on his staff. A twenty-six-year-old as a department head? Yes! This is the age of the Millennials and their brains and expertise are vital to the growth and relevance of business today. Since communication is critical to every business, a closer look at our multi-generational communication tools was a wake-up call to the Traditional Generation as well as to Baby Boomers.

"I have no recollection of ever writing a letter to someone and waiting for their response by mail," Natasha told me. As our bright and motivated twenty-four-year-old account coordinator, she related that she writes and receives over two hundred text messages a day, continuing to explain that it's more productive in scheduling, rescheduling, and planning her interactions with fellow workers, media reps, and clients. Natasha added that, when she was a ten-year-old, she started Instant Messaging on AOL, then moving on to G-Chat, and now to hundreds of texts per day.

> **Our group meetings are briefer and fewer, with email and text updates replacing the face-to-face "sit-downs" that used to sap valuable time.**

Awni, our twenty-eight-year-old video manager, uses Facebook Messenger as his most trusted way to ensure that the recipient gets his messages. His colleagues continually check their open Facebook message chat box and get Facebook message notifications simultaneously on their cell phone. Awni moonlights as a stand-up comic (he's good!) so sending his video demo reel using YouTube, through Facebook Messenger, is his easiest communication platform. Awni's customized cell phone plan allows for the fewest possible minutes of phone time, but unlimited texting. It works for him.

Andres relies on email solely for business communication and to send and receive urgent documents. His Facebook Chat Box gives him minute-to-minute access to his network, personally and professionally. No newspaper front page for Andres. He clicks on Twitter each morning for his news and celebrity updates. He ranks Facebook, Instagram, and Twitter as his primary methods of communication.

For Gen-Xers and Millennials, sharing with others enhances the experience, whether it's a day at the beach or a sushi dinner. Instagram, originally an app tool for artists and photographers, has gone mainstream, as has Vine, owned by Twitter. The seven-second video clips on Vine have taken sharing to a whole new level.

About five years ago, I left a meeting with Court, our president, where we agreed to find and hire a new art director and a new video producer. I was about to ask him how to phrase the classified ad when I saw him turn to access Facebook on his computer. "This is where I find the best talent and know their abilities before they walk in our front door," he told me. "I also hired our last copywriter from our website's 'contact us' page. And the best job search resource is right here in our office, with everyone's Facebook, LinkedIn, and Twitter activity."

The upside is that it's easier for an employer to match and marry the right talent and capabilities to the job opening. The downside is that many skilled and talented workers in the Baby Boomer generation are not fully utilizing cross-platforms of social media, and may not be the first point-of-contact for a prospective employer.

For small businesses without a robust HR department, the most productive methodology for finding good people is implementing a mix of online, traditional, and social media searches to find the right person at the right time.

It's far easier for four generations to integrate their work styles, disciplines, and communication methods, when each person recognizes and embraces their differences and evolves and adjusts to effectively reach the same objectives and goals.

Four Years Later: Stay or Go?

"To be successful, you have to be selfish, or else you never achieve. And once you get to your highest level, then you have to be unselfish. Stay reachable. Stay in touch. Don't isolate."

Michael Jordan

FOUR YEARS OLDER AND FOUR years wiser, with my buy-out payments behind me, I asked myself, "Could I envision years ahead of growth and accomplishments, or were the most productive days behind me? Did I still feel the need for that adrenaline rush of new clients and new profits, or was it time to turn in my keys and walk out the door for the last time?"

Being the eternal optimist, 80 percent of my brain pushed me to remain an important component of the success story. The tipping point was that 100 percent of my heart wanted to remain with our still-expanding firm. So I went with my heart.

In corporate America it's never easy to renegotiate a new contract when you're in your late sixties. Despite the ongoing conversation about anti-age discrimination, the mindset of senior executives is that youthful energy best serves the future destiny of the country's business sector.

In preparation for what I hoped would be a long-term successful contract negotiation, I focused on four words: Reinvent. Evaluate. Evolve. Reinvest. My goal was to remain Chairman of Green Advertising, now diversified into three companies: GreenAd.com; Orlando, FL-based Stalder/ Green Advertising; and our new video production facility, VidPop Productions.

Clearly we were not the same business that WPP Group had acquired in 1999. As our president, Court McQuire, often stated, "The advertising world has changed more in the last five years than the previous fifty years."

The first step was to painfully evaluate my relevance to our new business model. With little experience of social media, it was time to dig in and become knowledgeable and comfortable with my Facebook page, Twitter account, SEO methodology, blogs, and organic content. I thought I was computer savvy but soon realized I had a long way to evolve into mastering today's ever-fluctuating world of Instagram, Pinterest, Yelp, FourSquare, and more. Knowing the lingo and being comfortable with today's online communication skills were important, but understanding social media's relevance to the improvement of the operating profits of any company was crucial. This understanding ranked highly in proving one's executive worth in any company, but ours in particular.

As I reinvested time and energy to my first passion, residential real estate development, it was clear that the landscape had changed. Many renowned national home builders no longer existed. Now venture capital groups often provided funding for new developments. New players emerged with deep pockets to build their asset portfolios. With Google and Yahoo as my research tools, it became easier to build a "hit list" of regional real estate investment groups for multi-family housing, single-family housing, and condominium development.

I aggressively networked with these firms as well as major developers and current South Florida landowners, many who still owned huge acreages of former farm land, but had chosen not to sell during Florida's recent boom years. Perhaps my timing was good. Or maybe it was pure luck. The building cycle in our state was ripe for new communities and condominiums to satisfy the pent-up demand for "new housing" that had escalated in the previous years of foreclosures and short sales.

Meeting with new venture capital groups proved to be formidable. I brought Andres or Sergio with me, our bilingual account executives, since many of these high-level executives were more comfortable speaking in their native language, often Spanish or Portuguese. We were able to foster these new relationships that eventually led to the funding of new developments and consequently new business for our firm. People do business with people they trust and my phone began to ring with developers and funding groups who knew of my twenty-year success in marketing their business model. I'd hear, "Phyllis, you were there for the good, the bad, and the ugly. You know the minefields in our industry. Let's consult about some possible new projects now on our radar." Meetings and more meetings followed the early calls. It took almost a year, but these new connections bore fruit and added to our client roster.

Showcasing my relevance to the company's bottom line with emerging new business was the tipping point in my successful contract negotiations. Ten years later, I'm still here. Probably working harder than planned, but no complaints. It's all good.

Part Six

LET'S TAKE IT PERSONAL

The Art of True Connection

BEST-SELLING BUSINESS BOOKS WRITTEN BY successful authors can help polish your basic business skills and techniques. Speech coaches are enormously effective in teaching and reinforcing presentation skills and communication concepts. But the single, most important ingredient to business and personal success is developing your ability to connect with other people.

Let's start with the fact that most people do not have the ability to listen. I mean to *really* listen—not just wait until the other person takes a breath so you can readily respond. Or worse yet, interrupt that person because you know the answer and need to show how smart you are. The art of true listening has been greatly diminished as part of our communication skills, as has the ability to interpret body language and unspoken thoughts. I call true listening an "art" because it takes talent, dedication, and practice.

Early on I realized that the first and most important step to solving an employee problem was often to let the person talk. And talk and talk until they were finished (and often exhausted). Surprisingly, the more they talked, the closer the conversation evolved to a solution that we could both agree upon.

In all cases, the most powerful connection has always been the one-on-one conversation. Sadly, this has been replaced in our current business model by texts, emails, and more. It's often effective to take a step back and continually reinforce and remember the power of a personal connection.

In today's whirling world of social media, texts, apps, and pins, even the occasional telephone call is considered a pre-historic practice. But the personal connection still lives on. When you do have the opportunity to meet and greet a stranger, a vendor, a competitor, or a colleague, maximize that minute and make that connection memorable for both of you! Years later, that single connection could open the door to a new opportunity.

The Senator and the Lunch Date

W HEN YOU FIND YOURSELF SEATED across the airplane aisle from a famous U.S. Senator and a world-renown author, it takes courage and "chutzpah" to speak up and start a conversation.

It takes even more courage to offer Senator Ted Kennedy and his niece, Kathleen, then Maryland's Lieutenant Governor, a ride to their next destination in my bartered town car. I did both within a few hours, and developed a connection with Senator Kennedy that lasted many years.

I was straddling the worlds of selling for Paul Simon's radio station in Hampton Bays, Long Island, and the daily challenges of Barter Advantage on the Upper East Side of New York City. What could be more logical than creating a barter situation with Montauk Airways, the regional airline flying a daily route from New York's Marine Air Terminal to the East Hampton airport? With the promise of free radio commercial time, a smart executive at Montauk Airways signed a six-month barter agreement, and I found myself flying to East Hampton every weekend.

It was on a crowded sunny afternoon in June 1986 when

The famous and powerful have mastered the art and practice of returning favors, no matter how insignificant at the time.

my mother and I boarded the small commuter airplane at East Hampton airport for the short trip to New York's Marine Air Terminal. As we were seated, my mother, who had been visiting from Florida, turned to say, "Isn't that the handsome Senator Kennedy sitting just across from us? And that man with him looks familiar, too. I've seen him being interviewed on TV." Sure enough, it was the distinguished Senator from Massachusetts and he was talking to his seatmate, Carl Bernstein, the famous investigative reporter and author. And they were seated less than fifteen feet from us!

After briefly introducing ourselves, Senator Kennedy continued chatting with my mother about senior citizens' healthcare needs and how she was finding Medicare procedures in Florida. He was warm, friendly, and very nice. We landed two hours later than usual at the small Marine Air Terminal.

It was late and there were no waiting taxis. In fact the only waiting car was the bartered town car with a driver that I had reserved to drive us back to the city. I listened as the Senator and his niece, Kathleen, debated their options of how to get to nearby LaGuardia terminal to catch the shuttle leaving shortly for Washington, D.C. There were no options, and no aides to assist them in their dilemma. I carefully approached them, and offered to give them a ride in our waiting limo. Remember, this was way before security issues were on anyone's radar. And both Kennedys were still wearing the dressy attire from the East Hampton wedding that they, along with Carl Bernstein, had attended earlier in the day.

So there we were. With my astonished mother wedged between the Senator and the Lieutenant Governor in the back seat, with me sitting upfront near the driver. The fifteen-minute ride found them chatting non-stop, and ended with the Senator inviting my mother and a few friends to visit his private office in the U.S. Capitol in the fall. He graciously sent several autographed copies of his most recent book directly to her and her mah-jongg group in Florida.

After some memorable thank-you notes from the Senator's staff, I was invited to join Senator Kennedy for lunch at the Four Seasons in New York City later that year: just the Senator, two aides, and me. I learned that had the Senator not made the last shuttle flight to Washington that night, he would have missed a critical early-morning committee meeting with the President. During our lunch I told him of my plans to relocate to South Florida and go forward with a start-up marketing firm. He asked several key questions and offered encouraging and heartfelt advice.

I learned the importance of how the famous and powerful have mastered the art and practice of returning favors, no matter how insignificant at the time.

I remain impressed to this day.

The Masters of Connection:
Elizabeth Taylor and Bill Clinton

O VER THE YEARS I'VE MET many famous and powerful people in my career. Of all the politicians, show business personalities, and business leaders I have met, the two people who were true masters of connection were Elizabeth Taylor and President Bill Clinton.

I was fortunate to be seated next to Elizabeth Taylor at a Hollywood dinner where she shared the hosting honors with Melvin Simon, the late philanthropist and shopping center mogul. Bren, Melvin's wife, had insisted that I join them for the annual Simon Wiesenthal tribute dinner, since I was in town, visiting KABC-TV in Los Angeles.

It was amazing to observe so many celebrities gathered in a private room prior to the dinner. I was a nobody among some very famous people, and only there because of my friendship with Bren. Most of the stars were aloof, barely acknowledging my effort to introduce myself. This was not so for the one and only Elizabeth.

Elizabeth Taylor was charming…even friendly. She told me about her commitment to the Wiesenthal Foundation, and went on to tell me how strange it seemed being a senator's wife. (Ms. Taylor was briefly married to Senator John Warner at the time.) I felt as though I were talking to an old friend. We even talked about our children! And this alone was one of the unique qualities that made her so special. It was her down-to-earth, no-nonsense attitude and the ability to connect with people, despite all the years of the celebrity aura: the jewels, the illnesses, the men.

I learned that people who have the ability to make a connection with a stranger are always at ease with themselves. On a very different level, I promised myself that, in the future, I would try to connect with whomever I met, whether a hotel check-in clerk or an office receptionist or a taxi driver. Every person wants to be recognized by another and the human connection keeps us positive and focused in this crazy world.

I'll Never Forget Bill Clinton's Blue Eyes

W HEN YOU MEET A CHARISMATIC personality who happens to be an ex-president, you are impressed.

No, I mean *really* impressed.

Never overstate the importance of connecting with people in business. And I mean really connecting—not just shaking their hand and repeating their name. Most politicians have mastered the practice of connection. Master politicians have raised the practice to an art form.

I learned the true art of connection when I first met President Bill Clinton. I had met Hillary Clinton the previous year and found her to be charming, likeable, and approachable. Her husband, however, completely disarmed me.

I remember the day, time, and place when Bill Clinton looked into my eyes and told me what a privilege it was to meet and shake hands. President Clinton has the bluest twinkling eyes, and they truly bore into me at this particular private luncheon. In the two minutes that we conversed, he addressed me by name at least five times; he never lost eye contact; he shook my hand three times (with another hand on my shoulder.) After the photographer had his shot, I quietly heard a voice saying, "Next," which was my cue that our time was up.

And sure enough, the President was addressing the next guest in much the same manner.

Remember that every person wants to be treated like a VIP. We all want to feel important and respected. The personal connection is a business tool that is vastly underrated and much underused.

The Eternal Conflict: How Can I Do It All?

MOST WOMEN REMAIN CONFLICTED IN every area of their careers. "You can have it all, but not all at once," is the advice du jour for today's female graduates. In reality, much of this advice is also relevant for the new breed of the twenty-first-century male executive.

Sheryl Sandberg, Facebook's Chief Operating Officer, has written and spoken extensively about why women are not making it to the top, able to combine professional success and personal fulfillment. Her speeches often focus on the types of messages that working mothers should tell themselves and their daughters. One of her core points is that women continually underestimate their own abilities, resulting in a hugely disproportionate lack of women at the corporate-level suite or C-suite. She champions the concept that women do not effectively negotiate for themselves in the workforce. She tells women that the number-one business rule is to "Sit at the table." Be an integral part of the meetings and the conversations, not just an onlooker.

I obviously was unaware of Ms. Sandberg's advice during my earlier business start-up days. I was always determined not to be the "business woman", but to be the "woman in the business world." I first discovered gender bias in my earlier ABC-TV days. But as I struck out on my own, it was apparent that bankers look more at the bottom line than the "bottom" of a CEO. Show them profits, and they'll approve the line of credit.

Decades after the phrase "dual-career marriage" described working wives, with my early career aptly fitting that description, many women in private business or the corporate world still seek validation for their positions. Despite promotions and a successful career track, many women continue to feel insecure and lack self-confidence. It's not easy to transition from being the "dutiful daughter" in an apprentice role to an outspoken, confident leader.

Today, most women are hearing mixed messages: Own the room; speak up; don't subordinate yourself. Yet the real issue is the focus on gender. I never wanted gender to be the catalyst to my success. Portia Mount, a senior executive of Center for Creative Leadership recently noted, "Women tend to over-prepare, over-think, and over-analyze every opportunity and then it's gone. Sometimes the best way to learn and get the experience is to just jump in and do it! Project that confidence and soon it will become a part of you."

Another relevant gem of advice quotes Traci Entel, a top executive at Booz & Company: "To stand out and excel, especially as a woman in the business world, you need to lead. Think of yourself as a leader first, and then a designer or accountant or engineer second."

As I transitioned from "weekend weather girl" to network executive to small business owner, and finally to chairman of a WPP Worldwide division, I learned to stop caring so much about validation and what my current peers thought of me. I knew that very few would cheer for me as I passed them. If I had realized this truth in my early years, I would have taken even bigger risks.

Meet the TV Brats

FOR GENERATIONS THE LABEL OF "army brats" has identified the children of career military men and women. The traits attributed to army brats are the by-products of continual childhood moving experiences that result from the constant military career reassignments of their parents. The term is often designated to indicate the resilience and self-confidence mandated by the acclimation to a new home, a new state, a new school.

With a second home often being a TV studio or a director's control room, I affectionately referred to my children as "TV brats." From the time my oldest son Bob was four years old, he would spend Saturdays at a TV station, while I used the weekend hours to get a head start on the crash schedule of the coming week.

Bob's brother and sister, Steve and Suzy, were toddlers when they learned to look out for and avoid the thousands of cable wires found on the floors of every TV studio. For anyone who has visited a studio, the first rule is to always look down not ahead. That hasn't changed in fifty years. It's second nature to everyone in the industry.

As the star of his own TV show at the age of twelve, Bob didn't feel special or different. To him, it was similar to his brother, Steve, a star quarterback, playing in his high school's Saturday football game. When the NBC affiliate in Indianapolis auditioned talent for a new Saturday morning show, *Uncle Uri's Treasure*, it seemed natural for Bob to audition as the show's lead actor. He was awarded the lead role for the two-year run. The show, taped each Friday evening, would air the following Saturday morning, achieving huge ratings from an eager children's audience. It was nothing special to Bob, nor to our family. It was just another extra-curricular activity.

> For career working women, whether single or married, a well-nurtured family will mirror their success in the workplace.

Another local Indianapolis station planned to create a series relating to teenage crime, which was rising at an alarming rate. Steve's TV character experience where he portrayed a juvenile criminal was light years removed from Bob's character of a twelve-year-old hunting for weekly treasures. The PSA (public service announcement) was shot with thirteen-year-old Steve sitting on a bench in a jail cell behind bars. Steve was dressed in his high school football uniform, complete with helmet and a football. His crime? Shoplifting at a neighborhood convenience store. The message was straightforward: "Don't be stupid. Shoplifting is a crime. You'll not only miss the big game; you'll miss many chances in life because this one charge will remain on your record forever."

Steve was a terrific actor. He appeared forlorn, dejected, and rejected. It was a powerful message that resonated with the audience and won local community awards.

Suzy felt more comfortable in the director's console room, watching the fast-paced decisions on camera angles, camera cuts, and nonstop instructions to lighting technicians and prop crews.

The breathtaking action that determines every second of a live TV show can be a cliffhanger. TV audiences get a behind-the-scenes glimpse of these experiences watching shows like HBO's *The Newsroom*. My daughter's childhood experiences proved to be early training for her legal career, where courtroom drama far exceeds a scripted television show.

Years later, it was apparent that my TV brats shared the commonality of resilience and self-confidence found in the DNA of generations of our country's families of army brats.

It's critical to mold the family's unique situation so that each member develops individualism and self-reliance. For career working women, whether single or married, a well-nurtured family will mirror their success in the workplace.

A Business Plan for Your Family

THE BOTTOM LINE IS THAT many people need a plan to function in their dual roles as family member and business professional. There are multiple templates and websites that offer helpful advice on writing a business plan, and there are different methodologies for business plans for various stages of a company's growth: launch, credit needs, funding receivables, expansion and growth.

Business schools and classes teach us that a disciplined business plan defining objectives and goals can make the difference between success and failure.

Having raised a family of three very diverse children, living in four extremely diverse cities, I can testify that many of the tenets of a well-formed business plan will be equally adaptable if you create a business plan for your family.

A business plan for a family? Shouldn't a family be warm and nurturing and not raised according to a scripted plan? Well, yes and no. Today, the "cookie-cutter" family no longer exists. You know, the one where Dad goes to work; Mom stays home; the kids go off to grade school, high school, vocational school, or college. Each family is unique and individualistic. The commonality that most families share is that they live under the same roof until their children reach a certain age. Think of the remarkable generational differences of three, four, five, or more people sharing the same living space, but differing in almost every other aspect of their lives: food choices, music, friends, hobbies and sports, not to mention their Facebook and Twitter followings!

This business plan I'm proposing is not a focus on wealth distribution, allowances, healthcare, and education costs. Rather it's a plan that helps you write your own rules, recognize the short-term needs, and establish guidelines for long-term goals and dreams for each person in the family. Today's family is molded, not structured. The working mother is the artist, creating and developing a child or children who will thrive and mature with order and structure, while feeling nurtured and emotionally secure.

Involving your children in potential changes in their lives creates a sense of adventure rather than wariness about the future. In the pursuit of a meaningful career, I moved my family thousands of miles away from their homes several times. In the process, my children became less self-centered and more compassionate about others as they met strange classmates and made new friends many times over the years.

In Steven's junior year as captain of his soccer team at prep school, he befriended one of his star soccer players, Frankie Lung, an exchange student from Hong Kong. Frankie's family had arranged for his schooling and boarding with a local Indianapolis family. After soccer season was well underway,

Steven discovered that Frankie was living above a nearby Chinese restaurant in a small room with little heat.

"Mom, I have twin beds in my room. Can't Frankie move in with us for the next two years? He'll learn so much from living with an American family, and I promise he'll do his share of chores."

Steven's heartfelt enthusiasm swayed me, but it's never that easy. It took several weeks of communication with Frankie's parents, a Kowloon banking family, and then weeks to secure the school's confirmation. By Christmas, I was responsible for a fourth child. It was a learning experience for all of us.

Taking a page from the famous Kennedy family, we would use our dinner meal to hear a three-minute recap from each person at the table, of their day's activities and what they learned that day. Frankie, grateful for his audience, often took five to ten minutes to talk about his day's experiences and tell us about his childhood and family. Frankie and Steven became inseparable up to their graduation day.

I believe that few women who are mothers can achieve success in their chosen industry or profession without an accompanying feeling of family success and accomplishment when they arrive home each evening. The success I write about is not your child's acceptance at an Ivy League college (although that's great), or making the school's All Star sports team. The reward for molding your family is their growth into responsible adults who are keenly aware of the diversity in our world and the challenges to be conquered as they go forward on their own.

Our Family Business Plan

1. **Ensure that everyone knows what everyone else is doing.**

We kept a big white board in the kitchen with colored Sharpies for each child, outlining their schedules for after-school activities, sports, clubs, and religious school. Today, I would give each child a weekly computer printout of these schedules for themselves and for each of their siblings.

2. **Find time to eat together at least three days a week.**

Sounds easy, but it's not. Maybe it's a 7 a.m. breakfast instead of a traditional dinner. We would celebrate many birthdays over the years with breakfast blueberry muffins and candles if sports practice or Hebrew lessons interfered with the dinner hour.

3. **Communicate with each child, one on one, for ten minutes each day.**

Bedtime, when they're "stuck in bed" is best. There's no escape. They *have* to talk to you when you sit at the foot of their bed!

4. **Remember that in today's world there is no norm for what comprises a household.**

In *Lean In*, Sheryl Sandberg reminds young women to "marry the man who will be your life partner and share your values." Yes, having the right partner to share the responsibilities of raising a family is the ideal. Yet my years as a single mother were significant as a role model for my daughter, and as an example to my sons. In today's world there is no norm for what comprises a household. Tradition is what you make it.

5. **Allow for the unexpected and deal with it.**

Whether a child is eight or eighteen, they will find trouble. You'll be called to school after your son starts a fist-fight with his classmate during a school game; you'll find the police at your door after your teenager gets stopped for speeding; you'll discover empty beer cans that your fourteen-year-old carefully wrapped in a plastic bag and placed at the bottom of your garbage bin. It's not the end of the world. It's called growing up. Don't magnify the transgression. Communicate the consequences, determine the punishment, and then discuss it the next evening at the family dinner table.

Move On. Move Up. Move Out.

OUR FATHERS AND GRANDFATHERS (AND mothers!) welcomed longevity with one employer. Their loyalty was often rewarded with a rich pension plan or extended health and insurance plans. A career spanning forty years with one employer was considered quite the norm.

The seismic shift in corporate America's employment strategy reaffirms that in today's business climate, you work for only one person: you. And you only have two products to sell: your knowledge and your time. Whether you are self-employed or receiving a weekly payroll check, you are taking information from your brain and converting it to a product of value. Your worth should be directly related to your experience and knowledge in your occupation or profession.

In Marc and Angel Chernoff's book, *1,000+ Things That Happy and Successful People Do Differently*, they explain that knowledge alone is not power. "Knowledge is simply a commodity; it's a product like any other that has the potential to be sold. How knowledge is organized, packaged, presented, shared, and received by others is what makes knowledge so powerful."

Recognizing this concept, it's time to return to the branding message. You are a unique brand that begins with your DNA, your education, your life experiences, your career track, and the knowledge you have accumulated. You are a product with a definitive brand. How you package your brand to continually seek new opportunities is the difference between just getting by and taking action!

Fortunately, as many businesses evolve to fit the whirling speed of today's consumer, career opportunities to move up can be found literally in the next cubicle or office. In our company, yesterday's copywriter is today's blog writer and social media guru. Yesterday's layout art director is today's motion graphics director. People who quickly adapt to learning new skills continue to be relevant as they reinvent themselves and increase their power. Their power is strengthened along with the earning potential of their brand.

We thrive on good relationships. For those fortunate few, new opportunities develop in an environment where they already enjoy good chemistry with their colleagues. For most others, the challenge to advance and grow means moving up and moving out. It's important to recognize that change is never easy at any age. Action takes bravery and courage.

The recent college graduate enters a strange world of daily productivity. The young mother who returns to her career faces new challenges. The older worker with years of seniority senses a pattern of age discrimination. You might be moving to another company. You may be moving to another city. But when you make the decision to advance your career by moving on, moving up, or moving out, you are actually moving to a new and better life!

No Tricks to Getting Hired

I'D LIKE TO WRITE A few words regarding the fine art of finding the right position and making the right career moves.

As the current CEO of three companies, I have interviewed hundreds of job candidates over the years. I can tell you what I look for in an applicant and this advice may help those readers who want, or need, a new job—either now or during the lifetime of their career.

The employment situation is rather terrifying these days, with industry-downsizing, mergers, and mass layoffs. The average duration of unemployment for older people is over a year, compared with five or six months for first-time job-seekers. People can no longer depend on a career of training, promotion, benefits, and a pension.

All of these factors make the current job-seeking situation more complicated than ever before. First, there are recent college graduates seeking their first real job and willing to work for low pay and minimum benefits. Then there are the serious on-track career pros looking for more challenges and higher commensurate compensation. These folks may not be totally dissatisfied with their current situation, but they aspire to discover what else is "out there."

Lastly, there is the growing contingent of the "older" unemployed, widely considered to be the wrong age at the wrong time. This group has been advised by every self-help guru out there to do everything from having plastic surgery to increase their "youth appeal", to how to rewrite their resume, to the importance of seeking professional therapy. Susan Sipprelle, producer of the web site www.overfiftyandoutofwork.com, notes that she has stopped posting articles akin to "Five Easy Steps to get a New Job." The reality is, no matter what your age or status, there are *no* easy steps that lead to a company considering an individual for a position and then actually hiring that person.

Logically, the first step is to get the interview, which may be a telephone interview or an in-person meeting. So how do you do that? You do it by simply practicing the three Ps: patience, persistence, and professionalism. Know that your resume may get lost in a sea of online ad responses. Make your resume or CV as unique as you can. Realize that it may be "Who you know in addition to what you know." Follow the tried and true rules of dressing appropriately, writing follow-up emails or handwritten notes, and acting professionally. And know that you have to sell yourself and sell hard!

As a veteran interviewer, I am most impressed when the combination of energy and enthusiasm comes across.

Today we call it "self-branding." *Building Your Brand* is

the latest buzz word often used by career counselors to assist people in packaging and marketing their skills, their technical and professional capabilities, and their social marketing expertise. Then they are taught to network the hell out of every opportunity!

Some executives still fall back on the standard interview questions and probing queries such as:

"Tell me the truth about your childhood years."

"What's been your biggest career challenge and how did you handle it?"

"What's the *real* reason that you want to leave your present job?"

As a veteran interviewer, I am most impressed when the combination of energy and enthusiasm come across during the interview situation. Given that you are qualified for the position, the attitude and energy you show will go far in selling yourself as the best candidate. Skills can be learned; attitude cannot. Remember that when a job is posted or listed, the need precedes the body. In other words, the need to fill that position already exists. If you can sell yourself to the person interviewing you, then you are solving their problem.

And everyone wants their problems solved as quickly as possible!

Thousands and thousands of words have been written about clever ways to hire, trick questions to rattle a job candidate, and planned interruptions during the interview process. My advice is to always be prepared for the curve-ball that some executives still use. Just remember: you have only one chance to make a first impression. Use that one chance to showcase your brand and land that job!

Full Speed Ahead

"Every moment wasted looking back, keeps us from moving forward."

Hillary Clinton

FAILURE IS THE MOST BITTER, yet the best, lesson you can learn in life. From Steve Jobs to Jamie Dimon, the painful reality of failure or being fired forces many of today's most admired people to recognize their flaws and shortcomings before changing course to achieve accolades and success. As my personal journey unfolded, the lessons of authenticity and humility enabled me to acknowledge my weaknesses and vulnerability and take responsibility for going forward at the most difficult times.

Setting foot in Florida in the mid-1980s, after being fired from ABC-TV and floundering with a year's worth of freelance assignments, my immediate goal was to land a permanent paying job. I knew the world of television sales. I was an expert at converting business budgets to media placements. The four major TV stations in the Greater Miami area would welcome a pro with my credentials.

After making the rounds of every network and independent TV station in the area, I was granted the perfunctory first interview. Soon it was obvious to me that I was considered a has-been in the industry. Two twenty-something sales people could be hired at the same compensation range I was asking. I was a fifty-year-old woman who had a good run in the industry, but was unfortunate to be caught in the crossfire of a network sale with bottom-line ramifications.

After months of answering more ads and more interviews, I was forced to focus on writing the next chapter of my life. Feelings of being weak and victimized gradually diminished and my strengths evolved to being more powerful, resilient, and energized.

Years later, Nike said: "Just do it." I knew that before my fifty-first birthday I would create a start-up advertising and marketing firm. We would develop a USP that was unique to our size and our strengths. I didn't know how hard it would be. I didn't know the years of struggle that lay ahead. As I became more grounded in developing positive relationships in this new venture, I soon became aware that fulfillment would come, not just from a dream of success, but in the journey itself.

One of our greatest U.S. presidents, Franklin D. Roosevelt, said, "Happiness is not in the mere possession of money. It lies in the joy of achievement, in the thrill of a creative effort." These were great inspirational words, but the quote that best motivated me to work harder than I had ever imagined came from famous business success, Jack Welch, who said, "If you don't have a competitive advantage, don't compete."

Little Green Advertising had a competitive advantage. Me.

In June 1982, a few years before my career world crashed, I delivered a commencement address at Boston's Fisher College, which included these thoughts:

"The workplace roadmaps of the 60s and 70s are history, and for today's graduates, should serve only as guideposts to the future. Learn from this history. It will never change. But from today, forward, your life will never be the same. You will learn that to succeed in your career, and your life, you must, above all, be adaptable. Remember the past, but don't look back. You've learned from your mothers and fathers and you have continued your education for the past four years. Today you are leaving this auditorium with a degree that you've earned.

"Tomorrow you start on a new and untested path. Use your knowledge wisely. Find new roads. Write new signposts. Find joy and fulfillment and you'll be taking the first step to a successful life ahead."

My research for this commencement address was my own life.

Fifteen years later, I was still following this script.

I was determined to grow our small sub-chapter S start-up into a viable acquisition for one of the world's mega agencies. Today, with the average age of our employees hovering at around thirty, we have continued to deliver our unique USP with video studios, edit suites, green/screen rooms, social media, and website departments. We have astute, motivated account and media pros who recognize that the achievements of an organization are the results of the combined efforts of every individual.

Frustration or Success:
Three Personal Narratives

I T'S NOT WHAT HAPPENS TO you; it's how you deal with what's happened to you. How you handle the changing world is usually the difference between frustration and success.

Resilience and the ability to evolve are two of the most powerful attributes of successful people. We cannot control the many changes in our lives, but we *can* control our destiny. In earlier chapters I talked about my life's changes, and how I continued to follow a path that was dark at times, but still glowed with faith and optimism.

I have chosen to share the following narratives because they are the personal stories of three amazing women. These women didn't discover a cure for cancer nor have they run for the presidency of this country. What they *have* accomplished is how to succeed in life, each in her way. They have learned to remember the past and be adaptable to the present: to interpret new signals that direct their lives with fresh challenges and rewards.

Katie B. and her Story of Personal Change

"Dear America,

I suppose we should introduce ourselves: we're South Louisiana. You probably already know that we talk funny and listen to strange music and eat things you'd probably hire an exterminator to get out of your yard. We dance even if there's no radio. We drink at funerals. We talk too much and laugh too loud and live too large and frankly, we're suspicious of others who don't."

Chris Rose

LOOKING BACK ON ALL THIRTY-ONE years of my life, it's become apparent to me that I am a creature of habit, and possibly teetering on the line of OCD. This behavior is probably an excellent topic for the old "nature vs. nurture" debate. From birth I've been consumed with schedule and sequence. In fact, I grew up in New Orleans. In case you're not aware, let me explain that New Orleans is a city so set in her ways, that, despite a rapidly growing fast food industry, seven out of ten homes still slow cook red beans and rice on Mondays, because…well because we always have. I don't like change and I didn't come from a place where change was welcomed with open arms and a smile.

People talk about "defining moments in life," but to be honest, I never recognized the gravity of that statement until 2005, when my life was repeatedly permeated with those moments. On February 8th, Mardi Gras Day, I stood on the

> **It's not what happens to you; it's how you deal with what's happened to you.**

parade route surrounded by friends, laughter, and an overwhelming feeling of nausea. Even though the ground was littered with the usual two weeks' worth of Mardi Gras debris and mud, I actually considered laying down to make the world stop spinning—much as it can stop during a two-week-long party that is attended by the entire city and thousands of visitors.

I bid adieu to the crowd, found my way back to my apartment, and after a trip to the pharmacy and the longest three minutes of my life, I learned that I was no longer alone in the world. I was going to be a mother, and the world started to spin again.

At the time, I was finishing my last year of college, student-teaching a rowdy third-grade class, bartending five nights a week, waitressing the brunch shift at a popular restaurant on weekends, and attempting to juggle a relationship with someone who was moving to Florida three months after graduation.

I didn't have time for change, especially not change of that magnitude. But change was inevitable. What followed was a five-month-long string of shouts, tears, and reflection, before I finally packed up my tiny two-door car, waved good-bye to my beloved city, and sobbed the entire sixteen-hour drive to my new home in Florida.

I spent a few months just trying to survive the humidity and heat as my stomach grew larger with every breathing

moment and I tentatively attempted to explore my new surroundings. I found myself comparing everything I encoun-
tered to New Orleans; I became angry that things weren't the
same. I was more than homesick. My entire life had changed
in such a way that I wasn't sure I could handle the difference. I spent hours on the phone with friends hearing about
the molasses-slow way life progressed back home in New
Orleans. The more I heard, the more miserable I became. I
closed my eyes and pretended I could magically transport
myself back to the old days.

As summer in Florida continued, so did the unforgiving
heat and in turn, one of the most active hurricane seasons
ever—with twenty-eight tropical storms, fifteen of which
become full-blown hurricanes. In New Orleans, you grow
up and hear how the city is shaped like a bowl, and one day
a big wave would come, and wash everyone away. But because the folks there don't like change, including evacuating
to higher ground, the tradition is to board up your windows,
mix up a batch of Pat O'Brien's Hurricane mix, add extra
rum, and then sit on your porch with your fist shaking in the
air, daring "a lil' rainstorm" to mess with tradition. We call
this a hurricane party.

Hurricane Katrina formed over the Bahamas on August
23, 2005, and strengthened to a Category 5 over the warm
Gulf waters. Normally, I would be leading the hurricane
party, and heading to the store to get the usual supplies:
booze, batteries, and whatever perishable foods Dorignac's
had on sale because the power would definitely go out. This
time, I was sitting on the cold tile floor in Florida, wearing an
ill-fitting maternity dress, pleading with friends back home

to get out. By Sunday night, I had compiled a list of family and friends, categorized by the city to which they chose to evacuate.

The storm hit New Orleans the morning of August 29th, one month before I was due to have my son. I sat on the edge of the sofa and silently cried as I watched reporters rattle off cliché statements and statistics about hurricanes, while New Orleans drowned in the background. I won't belittle the days that followed by recounting tales of my couch crusades that violently tumbled between yelling at CNN, praying the entire rosary, and calling everyone, again, for a detailed status report.

Simply put, Hurricane Katrina changed New Orleans forever.

Time back there is now referred to as "before" or "post" Katrina, like BC or AD. But, just like with any hard time, the people of New Orleans found their way around it. Bars and restaurants opened first, to bring the residents home, and other businesses slowly started to follow. I won't say, nor will anyone else, that the city will ever be the same, because I honestly believe that Katrina made New Orleans stronger. It brought people together through faith, food, and a common conversation. I promise you that on any given night in New Orleans, around at least one dinner table or bar, there is a group of people gathered, swapping stories about that morning, and the many mornings that followed.

A few weeks later, at 4:55 p.m., I welcomed a screaming bundle of joy into the world. My dad was unable to come for the birth of his first grandchild because my parents had everything they owned crammed into a U-Haul truck in the parking lot of a crowded Holiday Inn in Beaumont, Texas. But my mom had arrived and was right by my side. I lay in the hospital bed, gazing into my son's eyes, while talking to my mom about what was to come. My son would never know the New Orleans that I grew up with. We guessed and speculated about what would change, or to what extent, but we never once spoke about how the people would change.

We knew that some things are constant and that faith is a funny thing.

I look back to those few months in 2005 often. I now have an incredible eight-year-old whose mere existence frequently shows me that there are times to throw schedule and sequence out the door, and accept change. However, as a New Orleans girl at heart, there are some things that will always remain the same. And that's OK.

Change has not only affected my life; it has, without a doubt, defined it.

Renate Urban: Life Is Too Short to Be Afraid

Change is good, especially when you have multiple interests and talents. People who do the same thing over and over for many years become undoubtedly very skilled and experienced, but they also become complacent. Complacency can lead to less motivation, less interest, and consequently less efficiency. Something new is refreshing and an invaluable stimulant. But change requires the courage to not just think about it, but actually do it. Self-induced planned change is the most wonderful thing you can ever do for yourself. But in reality, change is generally triggered by an outside stimulus and is therefore seldom perceived as good.

It's easy to become stuck in the daily grind. You think you're not ready for change, or you're just scared of its consequences. These feelings of fear and complacency can hold us all back and prevent us from experiencing the wonderful healing powers of change. Personally, I'm not a stranger to this scenario. It has taken me more than twenty years in the corporate world in various positions to realize my true professional and personal potential.

When I was a teenager, my parents, relatives, and teachers would often ask what my career goals were. My spontaneous answer was, "I want to work with languages, help others learn and understand, and I want to travel the world." Their disapproval was obvious from the frown on their faces. I grew up believing I had to consider a better path.

After much deliberation, my parents finally allowed me to study languages. Only then did I realize that being a language tutor and translator isn't very lucrative. In addition I thought I might be looked upon as someone who couldn't study a "proper subject" culminating in a professional degree and job such as a doctor, lawyer, or banker. Feeling continual pressure, I earned my business degree and pursued a career in international public relations and marketing. I was fortunate to work both in Germany and throughout Europe for many different corporations.

Everyone surrounding me was proud of me, but I wasn't happy. I still wanted to be a language teacher or behavioral coach, so I transitioned to the field of human resource training and development. Realizing that I most enjoyed being a trainer, coach, or facilitator, I kept visualizing myself as a trainer for a communication skills company or language school.

Although I realized I didn't need anyone's approval and I had always dreamed of owning a language school in Scotland, it still seemed a highly unrealistic goal to me. Then after years of searching, I was offered a job at a prestigious language school in England. It wasn't Scotland and it wasn't my school, but it was a first step and I couldn't have been happier! Any kind of change can be a catalyst to more change, and it didn't take long to discover an even better opportunity and to become more involved in language and intercultural training.

I was pursuing my dream of becoming an independent language, communication skills, and intercultural trainer, but I was still working for

Change is good. Face it. Embrace it. Do it.

a training organization. I just didn't have the guts to take the next step. I had the knowledge and the talent, but I was held back by fear and complacency.

Finally, yet another change in life allowed me to focus on my real career choice. When my husband and I moved to Florida, I knew this was my opportunity to start fresh. Aware that my educational background, skills, and the experience gleaned from living and working abroad would be highly valued in this country, it was easier to form a start-up business. There was a need for services I could provide and an opportunity to start anew as an independent contractor.

I was able to transition to founder and owner of Urban Training and Services, Inc., and I'm now extremely proud and happy that I have accomplished my dream. I knew what I wanted to do even as a child, and this dream has become crystallized today. I'm doing what I've always wanted; I just didn't know *how* to do it until I lost my fear.

It takes time and courage to pursue your unique vision and embrace change as a means to realize your dreams. Change is good. Face it. Embrace it. Do it.

Life is too short to be afraid!

Judy Wachs: Her Middle Name Is Resilience

WE WERE ALWAYS KNOWN AS "the Miller Girls", three very different female personalities, yet continually strengthened by the bonds of sisterhood.

Our oldest sister, Alma, was the responsible one, as most elder children are. It may not be in their DNÅ, but it seems to be their destiny to be a role model for their younger siblings. I was the independent Miller girl, the middle child who forges her own path without seeking parental guidance. Our youngest sister, Judy, long considered the baby of the family, surprised the world by growing up to be adventurous, daring, and fearless. Her life has been filled with daunting changes that would have derailed most women. In a nutshell, my sister Judy is the most resilient person I know.

In her early thirties, with four young children, Judy and her husband evaluated their life and decided that raising a family in their rural Pennsylvania home left much to be desired. They sold their home, bundled up their children, loaded their station wagon, and set their course for California. This was in the 1970s, far past the California "gold rush days" of a century ago. Who drives three thousand miles from home without the promise of a job, or a new home? Well, they did. Deciding that San Francisco would be their destination to build a new life, they bravely followed a roadmap of hope and optimism.

Judy saw opportunity where others saw only challenges. Using her educational background and common sense skills, she opened her Union Street office as a therapist and counselor. Marriage problems? Smoking issues? Gay/straight advice? Finding the path to her downtown San Francisco office was often a patient's first step to solving their problems.

At the time, Silicon Valley start-ups and job opportunities were still in their infancy. Judy never harbored doubts; instead she saw an opportunity and this time it would be more lucrative. She became the owner and first employee of a new executive search firm, one dedicated to finding brilliant, talented executives and techies who could fill positions in this newly exploding technological phenomenon. For years, her name was on speed dial for companies that needed immediate talent searches but wished to remain anonymous. Judy's skills in negotiating contracts and assignments made millions for her clients. Her business flourished as well, but her zeal and enthusiasm for the West Coast lifestyle was slowly diminishing. Her dreams of spending days and nights living the fast-paced, energetic New York lifestyle became more vivid. "I've already moved across the country once and learned to survive and thrive in a new situation. I can do it again," she told her incredulous family.

To those who have moved to new cities, new situations, and new homes, not by choice, but by a family need or an illness, it may seem irrational for a woman in her late forties to consider another dramatic move. As for her husband of twenty years, the word *amicable* deserves a capital A describing their divorce. To this day they remain best friends, sharing the experiences of their children's and grandchildren's lives.

As defined in an earlier chapter, making the choice to change your life's direction can be exhilarating, educational and empowering. You've chosen your path. You are writing your own history.

Judy's odyssey continued from her initial move to New York's Greenwich Village, to a home in East Hampton, then back to New York City's Upper East Side. Researching the residential real estate climate, she braced herself for another opportunity. Quickly leasing a Madison Avenue office, she boldly jumped headfirst into the tsunami of the city's real estate frenzy.

> **Empowerment is fueled by self-made decisions. Inertia can be your enemy. Change can be your best friend forever.**

In the country's number-one city, the powerful and successful residential brokers had a stranglehold of contacts within the large segment of affluent domestic and foreign buyers. The fight for lower-priced real estate sales by smaller independent brokers often became scurrilous and cutthroat. With perseverance and stamina, Judy knew she could eventually make it to the big leagues. But after a particularly harsh and chilling eastern winter, the appeal of a California lifestyle once lived brought clarity that would newly determine her destiny. She announced to her family and to the world that she was ready for another change, another challenge.

Living today in balmy Santa Cruz, my sister is an accomplished writer with articles published in *The New York Times*, read on the local PBS station, and discussed in college classes. At the same time, she renewed her executive search talents to integrate with her own best interests.

Empowerment is fueled by self-made decisions. Inertia can be your enemy. Change can be your best friend forever.

others. To earn the support of their spouses... "My husband... for both of us to... Green says. "And... self-reliance."... ated some of the... "But now we... and I will come... Ms. G... ned with... "I th

The Finest Course Ever Charted

WIN STAR

d, where
at Textron
the strong support of the
lifestyles succeed. "M
opportunity for b
a team." M
nder

career has made my children much stronger,"

Works in New York but Boston is home away from their childr

As m
home, Ms. Barkley an
are particularly conce

and inflation.
creator, said the
ranging from wills
investment clubs,
retirement planning
laws.
timeliness of all *Money*
the-minute features

second quarter
debut another new
Report.
Because 20 department stores already
sponsor *Fashion Report* getting the
business from the "whole other half of the
store is a logical extension," Green
explained.

as host. He must have credibility, and
host should be a writer as well," Gre
explained.
Another series of new infomercials,

Acknowledgements

I F ANYONE BELIEVES THEY CAN write a book without a brilliant editor, I'd like to talk to that person. I love to write and considered my writing a meaningful pastime. I had managed to write a few early chapters, more as a hobby than a consequential endeavor. My life changed the day I met Margarita Pardo Abrishami. I confided to her that I loved writing about my experiences and how they shaped my life. She bluntly told me, "You should write a book," and she was right. Margarita, an accomplished editor and publisher, gave me the structure, confidence, and encouragement that I was lacking. She focused on turning my personal story into a documented journey to which others would relate. With her patient guidance, my story became a journey of survival.

My life has been enhanced by the love of family members who have shared many chapters of my journey: my godson Kenny Krichman, my nieces Brinda and Kelly, and my nephews Greg and Joe. You learned about my warm and close relationship with my sister Judy when you read the chapter describing her unbounded resilience.

I also acknowledge my "second" family: the skilled and talented colleagues at Green Advertising who played an integral role in the publication of this book. Octavio Guzman is the genius who designed the book's cover. Octavio gives words a visual meaning; he's the best in the business. Our website came alive when Sergio Melicio, with his Brazilian energy and enthusiasm, designed this critical component. Jeannie Schnurr's can-do attitude and advice were integral to completing all the initiatives on target and on time.

Pete Shepard and Andres Sanchez assisted me in numerous functions to complete the document and implement key social media communication platforms. Donna Golden-Uliano's ongoing support continually inspires me. The talented Jamie Rodriguez provided artistic context with his imaginative sketches. Court McQuire's loyalty and focus helped me navigate choppy waters over the past two decades. Now our company continues to flourish. WPP's succession plan is successful. We will always be in good hands with Court's leadership.

About the Author

P HYLLIS GREEN STARTED HER CAREER at a small 250-watt radio station in Trenton, New Jersey. Her first leap to a major market catapulted her to a 100,000-watt station in Miami, Florida. As she focused on steady, upward advancement in the broadcast industry, the position of Promotion Manager/Weekend Weather Girl at a Miami TV station initiated the launch of her television career.

After four years as a producer at the ABC-TV affiliate in Indianapolis, she seized the opportunity to capitalize on her broadcast skills by creating a new position of Media Manager at a large chain of retail department stores headquartered in the city. This proved to be exceptionally fortuitous, as just a few years later, large TV networks sought out those few professionals who could navigate the disparate worlds of broadcasting and retail advertising.

Serving first at the NBC-TV affiliate in Boston, and then joining ABC-TV in New York, Phyllis was a pioneer in creating and developing retail advertising campaigns throughout the country. Yet after the Capital Cities acquisition of ABC-TV, her world changed overnight. She was fired.

Phyllis decided to become an entrepreneur. Forming Green Advertising in 1986 offered her a unique challenge: to merge her sales, production and advertising skills to build a small business. This sub chapter-S corporation would grow to become one of the most respected advertising agencies in the state of Florida.

Green Advertising continually expanded its client base and billings through the 1990s, and was named by *Florida Trend* magazine as one of Florida's 100 Fastest Growing Companies. By 1999, Green's growth led to the firm's acquisition by WPP Worldwide, the world's largest marketing and communication agency. Presently, Phyllis Green serves as Chairman of Green Advertising, the parent company of GreenAd.com; Stalder/Green Advertising in Orlando, and VidPop Productions, video production complex in Boca Raton.